D0795626

HD WORD

Student Workbook
Units 21–33

REALLY GREAT READING

Really Great Reading

PO Box 46
Cabin John, MD 20818
1-942598-19-X

www.ReallyGreatReading.com

Curriculum Development Team:
Janeen Hergert, M. Ed., Amy E. Vanden Boogart, Ed.D., Kathy Young, M. Ed., Dara Wagner, M. Ed.,
Traci Birge, M.A., Claudia Martín, MST

Graphic Design:
Ingrid Shwaiko, Nichole Monaghan

First Edition
978-1-942598-19-0
194259819X AGS0621

AGS, an RRD Company
White Plains, MD USA
June 2021
25860

Printed in the U.S.A.

▶ Table of Contents

Reader 1: _____   Date: _____

Reader 2: _____

Reader 3: _____

Words to Preview	Point & Say

1 **tuber** – a short, thick stem that grows under the ground.
A potato is a tuber.

2 **fertilize** – add natural or chemical substances to make the soil better for growing crops.
The farmer wanted to fertilize the soil so he could grow a large crop.

3 **mature** – to become ripe or fully developed.
Some vegetables mature more quickly than others.

4 **famine** – a drastic food shortage that affects a large area.
Many people died during the famine that struck several African countries.

Point & Say

vitamins

minerals

fiber

Ireland

Potatoes

Note: Hyphenated words count as one word.

READER 1

The potato is a vegetable. About 80 percent of a potato is water. The rest	15
is made of vitamins, minerals, and fiber. These are things that make foods	28
healthy to eat and help young people to grow.	37
Potato plants are bushy, with dark green leaves and small flowers. The	49
plants can grow up to three feet tall, but the potatoes themselves do not	63
grow above the ground. Potatoes are tubers, which are roots that grow	75
under the ground. They store energy in the form of food.	86
Potatoes can be a variety of different colors. They can have white,	98
brown, red, blue, or purple skin. The inside of potatoes is usually yellow	111
or white.	113

READER 2

Potatoes also have different shapes and sizes. Some potatoes are round,	124
and others are closer to an oval shape. The smallest potatoes weigh	136
about an ounce, but the largest weigh more than two pounds.	147
One potato plant usually produces three to twenty potatoes. The	157
number depends on the soil, the type of plant, and the climate.	169

Growing potato plants takes work. Farmers fertilize the soil to help their — 181
crops grow. They use machines to plant perfect rows of potatoes. They — 193
have to keep weeds and pests from harming the crops. — 203

Potatoes must be planted every year. It takes about 70 to 180 days for — 217
plants to mature. The vines must be brown before potatoes can be — 229
harvested. Farmers also use machines to dig up the potatoes. Then, — 240
they must be sorted and checked by hand. — 248

READER 3

Potato plants can grow in many areas, but they grow best when it is — 262
warm during the day and cooler at night. Farmers need to harvest crops — 275
before heavy frosts because cold weather can make it easy for potatoes — 287
to bruise. Cold can also cause potatoes to rot. — 296

People have grown potatoes for thousands of years. Potatoes were first — 307
grown in South America. In the 1500s, Spanish explorers took potatoes — 318
back to Europe. Before long, the potato was a common food in parts of — 332
Europe. They were a very important food in Ireland. — 341

In the 1840s, many Irish people depended on potato crops. Sadly, in — 353
1845, disaster hit the country. The potato crops failed because of disease. — 365
This was called the Great Irish Famine. Many people did not have — 377
enough to eat. Others got sick. More than two million people left Ireland — 390
or died. — 392

Potatoes are still an important food in Ireland. They are also eaten in — 405
most other parts of the world. People like potatoes cooked many ways. — 417
They like them boiled, fried, mashed, or baked. Cooks put them in stews, — 430
soups, and salads. — 433

Calculation Boxes

Number of Words at Bracket	Reader 1	Number of Words at Bracket	Reader 2	Reader 3
		Subtract: Number of Words at Subhead	-113	-248
		Equals: Number of Words Attempted		
Subtract: Number of Errors	–	Subtract: Number of Errors	–	–
Equals: Words Correct per Minute (WCPM)		Equals: Words Correct per Minute (WCPM)		
Accuracy Percentage	%	Accuracy Percentage	%	%

Reader 1: _____   Date: _____

Reader 2: _____

Reader 3: _____

Potatoes

Note: Hyphenated words count as one word.

READER 1

The potato is a vegetable. About 80 percent of a potato is water. The rest	15
is made of vitamins, minerals, and fiber. These are things that make foods	28
healthy to eat and help young people to grow.	37
Potato plants are bushy, with dark green leaves and small flowers. The	49
plants can grow up to three feet tall, but the potatoes themselves do not	63
grow above the ground. Potatoes are tubers, which are roots that grow	75
under the ground. They store energy in the form of food.	86
Potatoes can be a variety of different colors. They can have white,	98
brown, red, blue, or purple skin. The inside of potatoes is usually yellow	111
or white.	113

READER 2

Potatoes also have different shapes and sizes. Some potatoes are round,	124
and others are closer to an oval shape. The smallest potatoes weigh	136
about an ounce, but the largest weigh more than two pounds.	147
One potato plant usually produces three to twenty potatoes. The	157
number depends on the soil, the type of plant, and the climate.	169
Growing potato plants takes work. Farmers fertilize the soil to help their	181
crops grow. They use machines to plant perfect rows of potatoes. They	193
have to keep weeds and pests from harming the crops.	203
Potatoes must be planted every year. It takes about 70 to 180 days for	217
plants to mature. The vines must be brown before potatoes can be	229
harvested. Farmers also use machines to dig up the potatoes. Then,	240
they must be sorted and checked by hand.	248

READER 3

Potato plants can grow in many areas, but they grow best when it is	262
warm during the day and cooler at night. Farmers need to harvest crops	275

before heavy frosts because cold weather can make it easy for potatoes	287
to bruise. Cold can also cause potatoes to rot.	296

People have grown potatoes for thousands of years. Potatoes were first	307
grown in South America. In the 1500s, Spanish explorers took potatoes	318
back to Europe. Before long, the potato was a common food in parts of	332
Europe. They were a very important food in Ireland.	341

In the 1840s, many Irish people depended on potato crops. Sadly, in	353
1845, disaster hit the country. The potato crops failed because of disease.	365
This was called the Great Irish Famine. Many people did not have	377
enough to eat. Others got sick. More than two million people left Ireland	390
or died.	392

Potatoes are still an important food in Ireland. They are also eaten in	405
most other parts of the world. People like potatoes cooked many ways.	417
They like them boiled, fried, mashed, or baked. Cooks put them in stews,	430
soups, and salads.	433

Investigate the Text

1. Underline the sentence that tells **what percentage** of a potato is water.
   Write ① at the beginning of this underlined sentence.

2. Underline the sentence that tells **how many** potatoes usually grow on a potato plant.
   Write ② at the beginning of this underlined sentence.

3. Underline the sentence that tells **how long** it takes potato plants to mature.
   Write ③ at the beginning of this underlined sentence.

4. Underline the sentence that tells **when** the Great Irish Famine happened.
   Write ④ at the beginning of this underlined sentence.

Calculation Boxes

	Reader 1		Reader 2	Reader 3
		Number of Words at Bracket		
		Subtract: Number of Words at Subhead	-113	-248
Number of Words at Bracket		Equals: Number of Words Attempted		
Subtract: Number of Errors	–	Subtract: Number of Errors	–	–
Equals: Words Correct per Minute (WCPM)		Equals: Words Correct per Minute (WCPM)		
Accuracy Percentage	%	Accuracy Percentage	%	%

Mark It!

1. bel<u>ong</u>
2. chipmunk
3. rethink
4. boomerang
5. donkey
6. restrung
7. anklet
8. lifelong
9. cliffhanger
10. snowbank
11. inkblot
12. finger

Read It!

1. chipmunk
2. anklet
3. rethink
4. cliffhanger
5. boomerang
6. inkblot
7. belong
8. finger

finger
boomerang
inkblot
lifelong
donkey
snowbank
cliffhanger
restrung

snowbank
donkey
restrung
belong
chipmunk
anklet
lifelong
rethink

Write chunks and all vowel spellings in the correct columns. The *schwa* spellings are circled and filled in.

CHALLENGING

1. ⓐ•long
2. scout•ⓔd
3. frank•ly
4. cⓞm•plain

Chunk	Schwa	Short	Long	Other	R-Controlled
ong	a				
	e				
	o				

MORE CHALLENGING

5. skate•board
6. mus•tang
7. o•ver•think
8. pro•gram

Chunk	Schwa	Short	Long	Other	R-Controlled

MOST CHALLENGING

9. ex•plo•sⓘve
10. thank•fⓤl
11. mon•ⓞ•tone
12. coun•ter•sunk

Chunk	Schwa	Short	Long	Other	R-Controlled
	i_e				
	u				
	o				

CHALLENGING

1. a small trinket to remember me (6)
2. sang a tune like the pretty songbird (7)
3. likes to drink oolong tea with her bagel (8)
4. cannot pull the long bee stinger out of his finger (10)

MORE CHALLENGING

5. will slink away quickly if I ever encounter a skunk (10)
6. flung a thick fingerling potato to the pink kangaroo (9)
7. play ping-pong with the prankster in the clown costume (9)
8. did a tango, a conga, and the limbo at a swanky party (12)

CHALLENGING

1. First, find out if the subject of the phrase is singular or plural. (13)
2. Sandra never wore the anklet with the shiny mustang charm. (10)
3. The trunk of that oak tree is a hangout for a noisy woodpecker. (13)
4. Albert's old swim trunks shrank in the laundry, so he had to bring his newest pair. (16)

MORE CHALLENGING

5. Greta said she will bring me a boomerang from her yearlong trip around the world. (15)
6. When I awoke yesterday, I saw that snow had blanketed the embankment near my shed. (15)
7. Books with really good cliffhangers at the end of each chapter make me linger in bed a little longer. (19)
8. My cranky bunkmate at camp is finally in a better mood after hearing that we are eating pancakes for dinner. (20)

SENTENCES

1. Read each sentence.
2. <u>Underline</u> all of the chunks.
3. Circle the words that have a chunk **and** are more than two syllables.

1 A prankster connected all of the notes in the songbook before the Thanksgiving musical.

2 The lanky kangaroo sank down into the fuzzy blanket and rested.

3 I think I'll stop by the fishmongers to get some fresh halibut and longneck eel for the chowder.

CHALLENGE YOURSELF

Create **one** sentence with at least **three** words that rhyme with **sink**. Underline those rhyming words. For an extra challenge, try to include more than three rhyming words in your sentence.

_____

_____

_____

Reader 1: _____   Date: _____

Reader 2: _____

Reader 3: _____

Words to Preview	Point & Say

1 **protein** – an important part of the daily diet that provides energy. *Beans, eggs, and meats are good sources of **protein**.*

2 **St. Louis, Missouri** – a large city in the middle part of the United States. *St. Louis, Missouri is a city along the Mississippi River.*

3 **pods** – long, thin pouches that contain nuts, seeds, or beans. *We had to remove the peas from their **pods** before cooking them for dinner.*

4 **allergy** – a body's negative reaction to certain plants, animals, or foods. *An **allergy** can cause itching or make it hard to breathe.*

Point & Say

naturally

recipes

Peanut Butter

Note: Hyphenated words count as one word.

READER 1

Peanut butter is a popular food. It is healthy because it has protein. Some   14
people like it smooth and creamy, but others like it crunchy and chunky.   27

Peanuts are native to South America, which means that they grow   38
there naturally. Explorers from Europe found the peanut plant when   48
they reached the New World. They took peanuts to other parts of the   61
world. At first, peanuts were only used to feed farm animals. Then people   74
realized that they could eat them too. George Washington Carver   84
created new recipes for peanuts.   89

READER 2

Peanut butter showed up in the late 1800s. No one knows who first made   103
it. One story is that a doctor invented it. He treated people with no teeth.   118
They needed protein, but they could not chew meat. The doctor ground   130
peanuts into peanut butter, which people could eat without chewing.   140
By eating peanut butter, they could get the protein they needed.   151

C.H. Sumner was one of the first people to sell peanut butter. He sold it	166
as a health food at the 1904 World's Fair in St. Louis, Missouri.	179

It takes many steps to make peanut butter. First, farmers grow peanut	191
plants. They plant them in the spring, and then machines harvest the	203
peanuts in the fall. Peanut plants hang upside down to dry. Once they	216
are dry, machines pull the peanut pods from the plants. The pods are	229
then shipped to a shelling plant.	235

READER 3

At the shelling plant, a machine removes any dirt and sticks, and it also	249
sorts the peanut shells. Workers then remove the peanuts from the shells.	261
They clean the peanuts, and then they send the shelled peanuts to	273
a factory.	275

At the factory, workers roast the peanuts in ovens. Fans cool them after	288
they are roasted. Next, one machine removes the skin from the peanuts,	300
and another machine grinds them. Lastly, salt and sweetener are added	311
before the peanut butter is put in a jar and shipped to customers.	324

The most popular way to eat peanut butter is in a sandwich with jelly.	338
Some people like peanut butter with honey. Elvis Presley ate fried peanut	350
butter and banana sandwiches. Some people eat peanut butter with	360
pickles, with bacon, or even with potato chips.	368

People who have a peanut allergy cannot eat peanut butter because	379
a reaction from the allergy can make it hard to breathe. People with this	393
allergy must be careful every time they eat. They must be sure to avoid	407
all foods with peanuts or peanut oil. However, peanut allergies are rare.	419
Most people can eat peanut butter safely.	426

Calculation Boxes

	Reader 1		Reader 2	Reader 3
Number of Words at Bracket		Number of Words at Bracket		
		Subtract: Number of Words at Subhead	-89	-235
		Equals: Number of Words Attempted		
Subtract: Number of Errors	–	Subtract: Number of Errors	–	–
Equals: Words Correct per Minute (WCPM)		Equals: Words Correct per Minute (WCPM)		
Accuracy Percentage	%	Accuracy Percentage	%	%

Reader 1: _____ Date: _____

Reader 2: _____

Reader 3: _____

Peanut Butter

Note: Hyphenated words count as one word.

READER 1

Peanut butter is a popular food. It is healthy because it has protein. Some	14
people like it smooth and creamy, but others like it crunchy and chunky.	27
Peanuts are native to South America, which means that they grow	38
there naturally. Explorers from Europe found the peanut plant when	48
they reached the New World. They took peanuts to other parts of the	61
world. At first, peanuts were only used to feed farm animals. Then people	74
realized that they could eat them too. George Washington Carver	84
created new recipes for peanuts.	89

READER 2

Peanut butter showed up in the late 1800s. No one knows who first made	103
it. One story is that a doctor invented it. He treated people with no teeth.	118
They needed protein, but they could not chew meat. The doctor ground	130
peanuts into peanut butter, which people could eat without chewing.	140
By eating peanut butter, they could get the protein they needed.	151
C.H. Sumner was one of the first people to sell peanut butter. He sold it	166
as a health food at the 1904 World's Fair in St. Louis, Missouri.	179
It takes many steps to make peanut butter. First, farmers grow peanut	191
plants. They plant them in the spring, and then machines harvest the	203
peanuts in the fall. Peanut plants hang upside down to dry. Once they	216
are dry, machines pull the peanut pods from the plants. The pods are	229
then shipped to a shelling plant.	235

READER 3

At the shelling plant, a machine removes any dirt and sticks, and it also	249
sorts the peanut shells. Workers then remove the peanuts from the shells.	261
They clean the peanuts, and then they send the shelled peanuts to	273
a factory.	275

At the factory, workers roast the peanuts in ovens. Fans cool them after	288
they are roasted. Next, one machine removes the skin from the peanuts,	300
and another machine grinds them. Lastly, salt and sweetener are added	311
before the peanut butter is put in a jar and shipped to customers.	324

The most popular way to eat peanut butter is in a sandwich with jelly.	338
Some people like peanut butter with honey. Elvis Presley ate fried peanut	350
butter and banana sandwiches. Some people eat peanut butter with	360
pickles, with bacon, or even with potato chips.	368

People who have a peanut allergy cannot eat peanut butter because	379
a reaction from the allergy can make it hard to breathe. People with this	393
allergy must be careful every time they eat. They must be sure to avoid	407
all foods with peanuts or peanut oil. However, peanut allergies are rare.	419
Most people can eat peanut butter safely.	426

Investigate the Text

1. Underline the sentence that tells the continent **where** Europeans first discovered peanuts.
   Write ① at the beginning of this underlined sentence.

2. Underline the sentence that tells **where** C.H. Sumner sold peanut butter as a health food.
   Write ② at the beginning of this underlined sentence.

3. Underline the sentence that tells **when** peanuts are harvested.
   Write ③ at the beginning of this underlined sentence.

4. Underline the sentence that tells **why** some people cannot eat peanut butter.
   Write ④ at the beginning of this underlined sentence.

Calculation Boxes

	Reader 1		Reader 2	Reader 3
Number of Words at Bracket		Number of Words at Bracket		
		Subtract: Number of Words at Subhead	-89	-235
		Equals: Number of Words Attempted		
Subtract: Number of Errors	−	Subtract: Number of Errors	−	−
Equals: Words Correct per Minute (WCPM)		Equals: Words Correct per Minute (WCPM)		
Accuracy Percentage	%	Accuracy Percentage	%	%

Detective Work

Mark It!

1. bun<u>dle</u>
2. article
3. maple
4. jungle
5. readable
6. sparkle
7. needle
8. tentacle
9. unstable
10. crackle
11. multiple
12. doodle

Read It!

1. article	needle	jungle
2. bundle	readable	crackle
3. doodle	multiple	sparkle
4. maple	unstable	tentacle
5. jungle	doodle	readable
6. multiple	crackle	article
7. unstable	sparkle	maple
8. tentacle	bundle	needle

Write each syllable in the correct column. The *schwa* spellings are circled. The vowel sound in the Consonant-le Syllables is always *schwa*.

CHALLENGING

Closed	Open	VCE	Vowel Team	R-Controlled	Consonant-le
1 hur•dle					hur	dle
2 ta•ble						
3 ea•gle						
4 dim•ple						

MORE CHALLENGING

Closed	Open	VCE	Vowel Team	R-Controlled	Consonant-le
5 sub•ti•tle						
6 dwin•dle						
7 strag•gle						
8 gar•gle						

MOST CHALLENGING

Closed	Open	VCE	Vowel Team	R-Controlled	Consonant-le
9 scrab•ble						
10 pine•ap•ple						
11 ob•st@•cle						
12 tea•ket•tle						

CHALLENGING

1. is only rentable on cable (5)
2. sparkle and twinkle like the stars (6)
3. should handle the candle carefully (5)
4. jumps at the sight of a single beetle (8)

MORE CHALLENGING

5. will guzzle the soda in the glass bottle (8)
6. as flexible as a wet noodle after stretching (8)
7. sprinkle the pepper on the tasty pickle soup (8)
8. must be able to add multiple numbers together (8)

CHALLENGING

1. Do the complex rules of this new marble game baffle you? (11)
2. Have you ever seen a purple poodle leaping over a hurdle? (11)
3. The little box turtle had a hunk of pink bubble gum on its shell. (14)
4. It is unsafe to unbuckle your seatbelt while the vehicle is in drive. (13)

MORE CHALLENGING

5. "Bundle up and get out of the drizzle," sang the fickle old man with the fiddle. (16)
6. Are you capable of making an apple crumble before the harvest festival this evening? (14)
7. Poppy does not find it enjoyable to doodle in a notebook or nibble on a pineapple Popsicle. (17)
8. What a spectacle it was to see Caleb shuffle the deck of cards and drop them in the middle of the table. (22)

Draw a line to connect the syllables that will spell a real word. Write the whole word on the line.

1

spar	ple	**temple**
tem	gle	_____
has	kle	_____
sin	sle	_____

2

baf	tle	_____
driz	fle	_____
un	zle	_____
tur	cle	_____

3

brit	zle	_____
puz	gle	_____
strug	ble	_____
stum	tle	_____

4

pos*si	cle	_____
mul*ti	ble	_____
par*ti	dle	_____
han	ple	_____

5

bot	ble	_____
crac	tle	_____
mar	kle	_____
mid	dle	_____

6

can	cle	_____
hum	fle	_____
ar*ti	dle	_____
shuf	ble	_____

CHALLENGE YOURSELF

The /uhl/ sounds can be spelled in a number of ways. Read the words below. Some of the words include the /uhl/ sounds and some do not. Underline the letters that spell the /uhl/ sounds and then fill in the letters that spell /uhl/ on the lines below.

political   obstacle   symbol   whirlpool   tranquil

enamel   prevail   lawful   surreal   newsreel

1._____   2._____   3._____   4._____   5._____   6._____

Reader 1: _____   Date: _____

Reader 2: _____

Reader 3: _____

Words to Preview	Point & Say

1 cocoa – a bean that is used to make chocolate; a hot chocolate drink; also the powder made from cocoa beans.
Cocoa is a popular drink on a cold winter night.

2 bitter – having a sharp, unpleasant taste.
*Some people think coffee tastes **bitter** without sugar.*

3 Aztecs – a group of Native Americans who had an empire in central and southern Mexico about 600 years ago.
*At one time, more than 20 million **Aztecs** lived in 400 cities and towns.*

4 Mayans – (pronounced my-inz) a group of Native Americans living mostly in southern Mexico and Guatemala.
*The **Mayans** have their own language, which is named after them.*

vanilla

valuable

wisdom

Europe

Chocolate
Note: Hyphenated words count as one word.

READER 1

People around the world enjoy eating chocolate. They eat chocolate	10
candy bars and drink chocolate milkshakes. Chocolate frosting tops	19
cakes of all flavors. Today, chocolate foods are sweet treats.	29
Chocolate is made from cocoa beans, which are hard, small, and very	41
bitter. They do not taste sweet like a dessert. Chocolate foods are sweet	54
only because they have sugar added to them.	62
Cocoa trees first grew in the rainforest of the Amazon. The Mayans were	75
probably the first people to use the cocoa beans more than 2,500 years	88
ago. Cocoa beans were also used by the Aztecs.	97

READER 2

Cocoa beans were very valuable to the Aztecs. They used the beans as	110
money. They also used the beans to make a chocolate drink that was	123
bitter and spicy, not sweet. The natives liked the drink because it gave	136
them energy, and they believed it gave them wisdom.	145

In the early 1500s, explorers from Europe landed in Mexico. They met	157
the Aztecs, who shared their chocolate drink. The explorers took cocoa	168
beans back to Europe. The chocolate drink was soon a favorite food of	181
the royal court.	184

For many years, chocolate was only served as a drink. The cocoa beans	197
were mixed with sugar, vanilla, cinnamon, or other spices to reduce the	209
bitter taste.	211

READER 3

Over the years, people found new ways to use chocolate. Cocoa was	223
added to cakes and candy. In 1847, a British company made the first	236
solid chocolate to eat. The Swiss were the first to make milk chocolate.	249

Turning cocoa beans into chocolate is hard work. Cocoa trees, which	260
are actually fruit trees, grow in tropical areas. Cocoa beans grow in pods	273
on the trees. Workers cut the pods from the trees using knives on long	287
poles. The workers then cut the pods open and scoop out the beans.	300
The beans are dried and sent to the chocolate factory.	310

At the factory, workers clean and roast the beans, and then they grind	323
them into a paste. Machines separate the paste into cocoa butter and	335
cocoa powder. Next, workers add sugar and vanilla. Bakers use cocoa	346
powder for cakes and cookies. Candy makers use the cocoa butter. To	358
make milk chocolate, they add powdered milk.	365

Today, people prefer different kinds of chocolate. Some people like very	376
sweet chocolate, so they eat milk chocolate. This is the most popular	388
kind of chocolate. Other people like chocolate that is not as sweet,	400
so they eat dark chocolate.	405

Calculation Boxes

	Reader 1		Reader 2	Reader 3
		Number of Words at Bracket		
		Subtract: Number of Words at Subhead	-97	-211
Number of Words at Bracket		Equals: Number of Words Attempted		
Subtract: Number of Errors	–	Subtract: Number of Errors	–	–
Equals: Words Correct per Minute (WCPM)		Equals: Words Correct per Minute (WCPM)		
Accuracy Percentage	%	Accuracy Percentage	%	%

Reader 1: _____ Date: _____

Reader 2: _____

Reader 3: _____

Chocolate

Note: Hyphenated words count as one word.

READER 1

People around the world enjoy eating chocolate. They eat chocolate	10
candy bars and drink chocolate milkshakes. Chocolate frosting tops	19
cakes of all flavors. Today, chocolate foods are sweet treats.	29

Chocolate is made from cocoa beans, which are hard, small, and very	41
bitter. They do not taste sweet like a dessert. Chocolate foods are sweet	54
only because they have sugar added to them.	62

Cocoa trees first grew in the rainforest of the Amazon. The Mayans were	75
probably the first people to use the cocoa beans more than 2,500 years	88
ago. Cocoa beans were also used by the Aztecs.	97

READER 2

Cocoa beans were very valuable to the Aztecs. They used the beans as	110
money. They also used the beans to make a chocolate drink that was	123
bitter and spicy, not sweet. The natives liked the drink because it gave	136
them energy, and they believed it gave them wisdom.	145

In the early 1500s, explorers from Europe landed in Mexico. They met	157
the Aztecs, who shared their chocolate drink. The explorers took cocoa	168
beans back to Europe. The chocolate drink was soon a favorite food of	181
the royal court.	184

For many years, chocolate was only served as a drink. The cocoa beans	197
were mixed with sugar, vanilla, cinnamon, or other spices to reduce the	209
bitter taste.	211

READER 3

Over the years, people found new ways to use chocolate. Cocoa was	223
added to cakes and candy. In 1847, a British company made the first	236
solid chocolate to eat. The Swiss were the first to make milk chocolate.	249

Turning cocoa beans into chocolate is hard work. Cocoa trees, which	260
are actually fruit trees, grow in tropical areas. Cocoa beans grow in pods	273
on the trees. Workers cut the pods from the trees using knives on long	287
poles. The workers then cut the pods open and scoop out the beans.	300
The beans are dried and sent to the chocolate factory.	310
At the factory, workers clean and roast the beans, and then they grind	323
them into a paste. Machines separate the paste into cocoa butter and	335
cocoa powder. Next, workers add sugar and vanilla. Bakers use cocoa	346
powder for cakes and cookies. Candy makers use the cocoa butter. To	358
make milk chocolate, they add powdered milk.	365
Today, people prefer different kinds of chocolate. Some people like very	376
sweet chocolate, so they eat milk chocolate. This is the most popular	388
kind of chocolate. Other people like chocolate that is not as sweet,	400
so they eat dark chocolate.	405

Investigate the Text

1. Underline the sentence that explains **how** cocoa beans taste.
   Write ① at the beginning of this underlined sentence.

2. Underline the sentence that tells **who** probably used cocoa beans first.
   Write ② at the beginning of this underlined sentence.

3. Underline the sentence that tells **who** first made milk chocolate.
   Write ③ at the beginning of this underlined sentence.

4. Underline the sentence that tells **what** tool is used to cut the cocoa bean
   pods from the trees.
   Write ④ at the beginning of this underlined sentence.

Calculation Boxes

	Reader 1		Reader 2	Reader 3
Number of Words at Bracket		Number of Words at Bracket		
		Subtract: Number of Words at Subhead	-97	-211
		Equals: Number of Words Attempted		
Number of Words at Bracket				
Subtract: Number of Errors	−	Subtract: Number of Errors	−	−
Equals: Words Correct per Minute (WCPM)		Equals: Words Correct per Minute (WCPM)		
Accuracy Percentage	%	Accuracy Percentage	%	%

Mark It!

1. atten<u>tion</u>
2. furniture
3. explosion
4. lotion
5. lecture
6. revision
7. vulture
8. fiction
9. emotion
10. sculpture
11. location
12. division

Read It!

1. division	lecture	lotion
2. explosion	fiction	vulture
3. attention	sculpture	revision
4. location	furniture	emotion
5. vulture	explosion	sculpture
6. revision	attention	lecture
7. fiction	emotion	division
8. furniture	lotion	location

Underline the Latin chunks. Place a checkmark in the column for the sounds spelled by the Latin chunk in each word. The *schwa* spellings are circled.

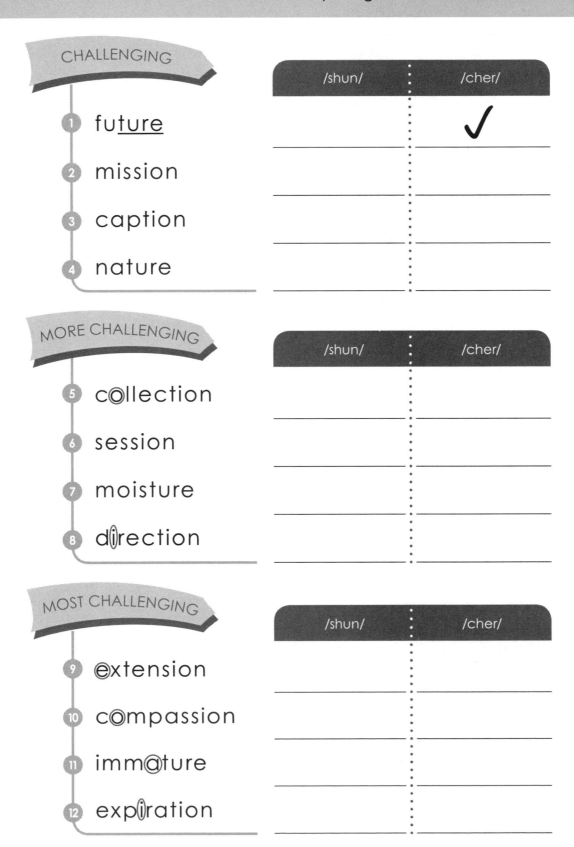

CHALLENGING

	/shun/	/cher/
1 fu<u>ture</u>		✓
2 mission		
3 caption		
4 nature		

MORE CHALLENGING

	/shun/	/cher/
5 collection		
6 session		
7 moisture		
8 direction		

MOST CHALLENGING

	/shun/	/cher/
9 extension		
10 compassion		
11 immature		
12 expiration		

CHALLENGING

1. lotion has a smooth texture (5)

2. must study a different culture (5)

3. agrees to pay for the optional feature (7)

4. ate a mixture of sweet and sour snacks (8)

MORE CHALLENGING

5. dislikes television programs without action (5)

6. will take a medication for her sinus infection (8)

7. needs to get permission to attend the auction (8)

8. should print the directions to the campsite location (8)

CHALLENGING

1. That scary creature under your bed is just an illusion. (10)

2. The jungle excursion was the best adventure of my life! (10)

3. I like the first version of the picture better because it is lighter. (13)

4. Eva has an objection to the tricky math equation on the exam. (12)

MORE CHALLENGING

5. Clover, my adorable dog, has a collection of squeaky toys that hold her attention. (14)

6. I will plant the yellow carnations in my garden bed as soon as the temperature rises. (16)

7. Margaret made a silly expression when she saw the sculpture of the fictional dog, Pluto. (15)

8. Your signature is needed on each version of the construction contract before the contractors can begin. (16)

WORDS

1. Read each word.
2. <u>Underline</u> words with the /cher/ sound.
3. Draw a box around words with the /shun/ sound.
4. Circle words with the /zhun/ sound.

signature	satisfaction	posture
revision	estimation	collection
equation	future	objection
capture	permission	adventure
discussion	nature	erosion

CHALLENGE YOURSELF

1 Find the two words that you might hear in math class.

_____   _____

2 Find the two words that you might hear in science class.

_____   _____

3 Find the word that means "a talk with someone." _____

4 Find the word that describes tomorrow, next week, or later.

_____

Reader 1: _____ Date: _____

Reader 2: _____

Reader 3: _____

Words to Preview	Point & Say

1. **kernel** – a grain of corn.
   Be careful not to break a tooth on a **kernel** of popcorn.

2. **hull** – the outer shell of a fruit, nut, or seed; the hard outer covering of a popcorn kernel.
   The **hull** exploded when the popcorn kernel got hot.

3. **headdresses** – coverings or decorations to be worn on the head.
   The women all wore beautiful **headdresses** for the Aztec history celebration.

4. **New Mexico** – a state in the southwestern part of the United States.
   We toured a deep cave on our trip through **New Mexico**.

5. **pressure** – force placed on something.
   David filled that balloon with so much air that the internal **pressure** caused it to pop.

Point & Say

Aztecs

Native Americans

Popcorn

Note: Hyphenated words count as one word.

READER 1

Why does popcorn pop? What makes the hard golden kernel explode	11
into the fluffy white popcorn we eat? Is it magic or is it science?	25
Farmers in the U.S. grow more corn than any other crop. Most of the	39
corn, though, will not pop. Only popcorn will pop. Popcorn is different	51
from other kinds of corn because it has a thicker hull.	62
Aztecs showed early explorers in North America how to pop corn. Other	74
Native Americans also ate popcorn or made soup with it. Some also	86
made jewelry and headdresses with it.	92

READER 2

There is proof that people have been eating popcorn for thousands of	104
years. In 1948, some very old ears of popcorn were found in a bat cave	119
in New Mexico. Some people think the ears of corn are about 4,000	132

years old. They may be the oldest ears of popcorn ever found. 144

Some Native American tribes thought that spirits lived in the kernels of 156
corn. The spirits were quiet and happy most of the time. However, when 169
their homes in the kernels were heated, they got mad. The hotter their 182
homes became, the more upset the spirits got. When the angry spirits 194
got too hot, they burst out of the kernel. That is when the corn popped. 209

READER 3

Science gives us a different reason for why popcorn pops. There is a 222
small amount of water in the center of each kernel of corn. As the kernel 237
is heated, the water inside it gets hot. The heated water quickly turns into 251
steam. As the water turns into steam, it expands. This puts pressure on 264
the hull. Finally, the steam bursts through the hull and breaks it apart. 277
The kernel turns inside out when this happens. The soft, white inside of 290
the kernel expands until it is filled with air. That is when the popcorn is 305
ready to eat. 308

There are many ways to cook popcorn. Some Native Americans heated 319
the kernels in bowls of hot sand. People used to sell popcorn that they 333
popped in a wire basket over a fire. Now, in places like movie theaters 347
and parks, workers pour the kernels into a popcorn machine. At home, 359
people use their microwaves to make popcorn in a bag. 369

People like to add different things to their popcorn before eating it. 381
Some early Americans ate it with sugar and cream for breakfast. Today, 393
people eat popcorn with butter and salt as a snack. Some stores sell 406
popcorn in many flavors. You can choose popcorn coated with cheddar 417
cheese, caramel, chocolate, or even grape. 423

Calculation Boxes	Reader 1		Reader 2	Reader 3
		Number of Words at Bracket		
		Subtract: Number of Words at Subhead	-92	-209
Number of Words at Bracket		Equals: Number of Words Attempted		
Subtract: Number of Errors	–	Subtract: Number of Errors	–	–
Equals: Words Correct per Minute (WCPM)		Equals: Words Correct per Minute (WCPM)		
Accuracy Percentage	%	Accuracy Percentage	%	%

Reader 1: _____ Date: _____

Reader 2: _____

Reader 3: _____

Popcorn

Note: Hyphenated words count as one word.

READER 1

Why does popcorn pop? What makes the hard golden kernel explode	11
into the fluffy white popcorn we eat? Is it magic or is it science?	25

Farmers in the U.S. grow more corn than any other crop. Most of the	39
corn, though, will not pop. Only popcorn will pop. Popcorn is different	51
from other kinds of corn because it has a thicker hull.	62

Aztecs showed early explorers in North America how to pop corn. Other	74
Native Americans also ate popcorn or made soup with it. Some also	86
made jewelry and headdresses with it.	92

READER 2

There is proof that people have been eating popcorn for thousands of	104
years. In 1948, some very old ears of popcorn were found in a bat cave	119
in New Mexico. Some people think the ears of corn are about 4,000	132
years old. They may be the oldest ears of popcorn ever found.	144

Some Native American tribes thought that spirits lived in the kernels of	156
corn. The spirits were quiet and happy most of the time. However, when	169
their homes in the kernels were heated, they got mad. The hotter their	182
homes became, the more upset the spirits got. When the angry spirits	194
got too hot, they burst out of the kernel. That is when the corn popped.	209

READER 3

Science gives us a different reason for why popcorn pops. There is a	222
small amount of water in the center of each kernel of corn. As the kernel	237
is heated, the water inside it gets hot. The heated water quickly turns into	251
steam. As the water turns into steam, it expands. This puts pressure on	264
the hull. Finally, the steam bursts through the hull and breaks it apart.	277
The kernel turns inside out when this happens. The soft, white inside of	290

| the kernel expands until it is filled with air. That is when the popcorn is | 305 |
| ready to eat. | 308 |

There are many ways to cook popcorn. Some Native Americans heated	319
the kernels in bowls of hot sand. People used to sell popcorn that they	333
popped in a wire basket over a fire. Now, in places like movie theaters	347
and parks, workers pour the kernels into a popcorn machine. At home,	359
people use their microwaves to make popcorn in a bag.	369

People like to add different things to their popcorn before eating it.	381
Some early Americans ate it with sugar and cream for breakfast. Today,	393
people eat popcorn with butter and salt as a snack. Some stores sell	406
popcorn in many flavors. You can choose popcorn coated with cheddar	417
cheese, caramel, chocolate, or even grape.	423

Investigate the Text

1. Underline the sentence that explains **what** makes popcorn different from other kinds of corn.
   Write ① at the beginning of this underlined sentence.

2. Underline the sentence that tells **who** taught early explorers in North America about popcorn.
   Write ② at the beginning of this underlined sentence.

3. Underline the sentence that gives the scientific explanation of **why** popcorn kernels break apart.
   Write ③ at the beginning of this underlined sentence.

4. Underline the sentence that describes **how** some early Americans ate their popcorn.
   Write ④ at the beginning of this underlined sentence.

Calculation Boxes

	Reader 1		Reader 2	Reader 3
Number of Words at Bracket		Number of Words at Bracket		
		Subtract: Number of Words at Subhead	-92	-209
		Equals: Number of Words Attempted		
Subtract: Number of Errors	–	Subtract: Number of Errors	–	–
Equals: Words Correct per Minute (WCPM)		Equals: Words Correct per Minute (WCPM)		
Accuracy Percentage	%	Accuracy Percentage	%	%

Mark It!

1. can<u>ce</u>l
2. allergic
3. gigantic
4. urgent
5. balance
6. pencil
7. luggage
8. digit
9. introduce
10. fancy
11. gentle
12. advantage

Read It!

1. allergic	fancy	introduce
2. advantage	pencil	cancel
3. luggage	balance	digit
4. gentle	urgent	gigantic
5. pencil	advantage	allergic
6. introduce	luggage	fancy
7. cancel	digit	balance
8. gigantic	gentle	urgent

Word Sort

If a syllable contains either the letter **c** or the letter **g**, figure out if it spells its hard or its soft sound. Write the whole syllable containing the **c** or **g** in the correct column. The *schwa* spellings are circled.

CHALLENGING

1. ⓔ•merge
2. i•cⓘ•cle
3. cir•cⓤs
4. ger•bⓘl

Hard c Syllable	Soft c Syllable	Hard g Syllable	Soft g Syllable
			merge

MORE CHALLENGING

5. gal•ley
6. cy•clⓘst
7. col•lⓔge
8. gro•cⓔ•ry

Hard c Syllable	Soft c Syllable	Hard g Syllable	Soft g Syllable

MOST CHALLENGING

9. ex•er•cise
10. dis•tⓐnce
11. en•er•gy
12. sug•gest•ing

Hard c Syllable	Soft c Syllable	Hard g Syllable	Soft g Syllable

CHALLENGING

1. can bend a pencil with magic (6)
2. the page with the wide margin (6)
3. has to recite each sentence twice (6)
4. is allergic to celery and spruce trees (7)

MORE CHALLENGING

5. the stage in the center of the college campus (9)
6. a scavenger hunt to find the largest Easter egg (9)
7. should apologize for your loud voice in the library (9)
8. a quick glance at the secret agent in the bushes (10)

CHALLENGING

1. Be very gentle with the fancy, glass icicle decorations. (9)
2. My mom drove to the grocery store just to buy gingersnap cookies. (12)
3. Grace, our pet gerbil, eats ice chips after she exercises on her wheel. (13)
4. Lucy and Nancy are about to embark on an exciting adventure in Iceland. (13)

MORE CHALLENGING

5. Please recycle the orange soda can rather than throwing it in the garbage can. (14)
6. Tracy suggested that we should do our research project on the culture of Greece or Egypt. (16)
7. Riding in the bicycle race will require a lot of energy, so eat some carbohydrates beforehand. (16)
8. Mice are nice, but they can carry germs that are harmful, so you do not want them dancing around in your cellar. (22)

WORDS

1. Read each word.
2. <u>Underline</u> words that contain a soft **g** sound.
3. Draw a box around words that contain a soft **c** sound.
4. Circle words that contain both a hard **c** or **g** sound **and** a soft **c** or **g** sound.

except	glance	magic
gargle	princess	accent
luggage	principal	ginger
policy	classic	orange
recycle	apology	cement

CHALLENGE YOURSELF

1. Find the two words that are flavors.

   _____   _____

2. Find the word that means "to use again." _____

3. Find the word that means "to look at someone or something quickly."

   _____

4. Find the word that describes something you might take on a trip.

   _____

Reader 1: _____   Date: _____

Reader 2: _____

Reader 3: _____

Words to Preview	Point & Say

1. **lumberjack** – a person whose job is to cut down trees and take them to the lumber mill.
   *The **lumberjack** worked hard yesterday and cut down six tall trees.*

2. **legends** – stories told over many years that may not be true.
   *Some **legends** are based on the actions of a real person, but the person's actions are made bigger than life.*

3. **tales** – stories about real or imaginary people or events.
   *We had fun sitting around the campfire while our scout leader told us scary **tales**.*

4. **axmen** – men who carry axes and help lumberjacks cut down trees.
   *The **axmen** helped cut firewood for the cold winter.*

5. **flapjacks** – pancakes.
   *On our camping trip, we cooked **flapjacks** over the campfire for breakfast.*

Point & Say: opera, exciting

Paul Bunyan

Note: Hyphenated words count as one word.

READER 1

Paul Bunyan is a famous lumberjack in American legends. Stories say he	12
was so big that he fit into his father's clothes when he was only one week	28
old! His voice was so powerful that he could clear the frogs off a pond	43
when he yelled. He was bigger and stronger than any real man could	56
ever be.	58
The stories about Paul Bunyan were first told by men in logging camps.	71
These men would tell tales at night. They always had Paul Bunyan doing	84
things that normal people cannot really do. The stories made Paul Bunyan	96
larger than life, or stronger and more exciting than regular people.	107

READER 2

Even tales about Paul's early years made him larger than life. When	119
he learned to clap and laugh, it shook the house so much that all the	134
windows broke. At three years old, he could chop through logs.	145

Many of the legends were about Paul and his ox, Babe. Paul found Babe	159
during a storm of blue snow. Paul took Babe to the fire to warm up. Babe	175
stayed the same blue color as the snow. He was big and strong like Paul.	190
They stayed together for the rest of Paul's life.	199

READER 3

Some of the Paul Bunyan stories are about the people he knew. He had	213
a group of seven axmen that worked for him. Paul named each of them	227
Elmer. That way, he only had to yell one name for all of the axmen to	243
come running to him.	247

Some stories are about the things Paul Bunyan liked. For example, Paul	259
loved flapjacks. He was big, so the pan he used to make flapjacks had	273
to be big, too. His pan was so big that he had to hire boys to grease it by	292
skating across it with strips of bacon strapped to their feet.	303

The tales of Paul Bunyan were first written down by a newspaper	315
reporter. That was in 1910. Since then, many other people have written	327
books about Paul Bunyan. These books turned this large lumberjack into	338
an American legend.	341

Movies, comic books, and even a small opera have been written about	353
Paul and Babe. Many towns in the northern United States claim to be his	367
hometown. Paul Bunyan is popular because he reminds people what it is	379
like to be big, brave, and bold.	386

Calculation Boxes

Reader 1			Reader 2	Reader 3
Number of Words at Bracket		Number of Words at Bracket		
		Subtract: Number of Words at Subhead	-107	-199
		Equals: Number of Words Attempted		
Subtract: Number of Errors	–	Subtract: Number of Errors	–	–
Equals: Words Correct per Minute (WCPM)		Equals: Words Correct per Minute (WCPM)		
Accuracy Percentage	%	Accuracy Percentage	%	%

Reader 1: _____   Date: _____

Reader 2: _____

Reader 3: _____

Paul Bunyan

Note: Hyphenated words count as one word.

READER 1

Paul Bunyan is a famous lumberjack in American legends. Stories say he	12
was so big that he fit into his father's clothes when he was only one week	28
old! His voice was so powerful that he could clear the frogs off a pond	43
when he yelled. He was bigger and stronger than any real man could	56
ever be.	58

The stories about Paul Bunyan were first told by men in logging camps.	71
These men would tell tales at night. They always had Paul Bunyan doing	84
things that normal people cannot really do. The stories made Paul Bunyan	96
larger than life, or stronger and more exciting than regular people.	107

READER 2

Even tales about Paul's early years made him larger than life. When	119
he learned to clap and laugh, it shook the house so much that all the	134
windows broke. At three years old, he could chop through logs.	145

Many of the legends were about Paul and his ox, Babe. Paul found Babe	159
during a storm of blue snow. Paul took Babe to the fire to warm up. Babe	175
stayed the same blue color as the snow. He was big and strong like Paul.	190
They stayed together for the rest of Paul's life.	199

READER 3

Some of the Paul Bunyan stories are about the people he knew. He had	213
a group of seven axmen that worked for him. Paul named each of them	227
Elmer. That way, he only had to yell one name for all of the axmen to	243
come running to him.	247

Some stories are about the things Paul Bunyan liked. For example, Paul	259
loved flapjacks. He was big, so the pan he used to make flapjacks had	273
to be big, too. His pan was so big that he had to hire boys to grease it by	292
skating across it with strips of bacon strapped to their feet.	303

The tales of Paul Bunyan were first written down by a newspaper	315
reporter. That was in 1910. Since then, many other people have written	327
books about Paul Bunyan. These books turned this large lumberjack into	338
an American legend.	341

Movies, comic books, and even a small opera have been written about	353
Paul and Babe. Many towns in the northern United States claim to be his	367
hometown. Paul Bunyan is popular because he reminds people what it is	379
like to be big, brave, and bold.	386

Investigate the Text

1 **Underline** the sentence that explains **how loud** Paul Bunyan's voice was.
Write ① at the beginning of this underlined sentence.

2 **Underline** the sentences that explain **why** Babe was the color blue.
Write ② at the beginning of these underlined sentences.

3 **Underline** the sentence that explains **why** Paul Bunyan named all of his axmen Elmer.
Write ③ at the beginning of this underlined sentence.

4 **Underline** the sentence that explains **how** Paul Bunyan greased his flapjack pan.
Write ④ at the beginning of this underlined sentence.

Calculation Boxes

	Reader 1		Reader 2	Reader 3
Number of Words at Bracket		Number of Words at Bracket		
		Subtract: Number of Words at Subhead	-107	-199
		Equals: Number of Words Attempted		
Subtract: Number of Errors	–	Subtract: Number of Errors	–	–
Equals: Words Correct per Minute (WCPM)		Equals: Words Correct per Minute (WCPM)		
Accuracy Percentage	%	Accuracy Percentage	%	%

Mark It!

1. point<u>less</u>
2. skillful
3. gladly
4. pretends
5. treatment
6. thickness
7. useful
8. motionless
9. gentleness
10. department
11. exactly
12. commits

Read It!

1. commits	treatment	motionless
2. exactly	pointless	useful
3. department	thickness	skillful
4. gentleness	pretends	gladly
5. useful	department	treatment
6. skillful	commits	thickness
7. pointless	motionless	gentleness
8. pretends	gladly	exactly

If you see a consonant suffix, underline it with one line. Some words do not have suffixes. Place a checkmark in the correct column. The *schwa* spellings are circled.

CHALLENGING

	Suffix	No Suffix
1. grace•f(u)l	✓	
2. per•m(a)•n(e)nt		
3. fi•n(a)l•ly		
4. sleep•l(e)ss		

MORE CHALLENGING

	Suffix	No Suffix
5. ar•gu•m(e)nt		
6. duf•f(e)l		
7. ac•cess		
8. ac•(tive)•ly		

MOST CHALLENGING

	Suffix	No Suffix
9. d(e)•pen•d(e)nt		
10. tea•spoon•f(u)l		
11. c(o)m•part•m(e)nt		
12. c(o)m•plete•ly		

CHALLENGING

1. ran swiftly on the snowless grass (6)

2. is grateful for the yearly subscription (6)

3. gladly took the peaceful weekend trip (6)

4. can hear clearly over the cordless phone (7)

MORE CHALLENGING

5. would normally have found a replacement (6)

6. had a delightful time at the amusement park (8)

7. a limitless supply of flourless chocolate cupcakes (7)

8. like the crookedness of the maple tree in the yard (10)

CHALLENGING

1. The cuddly baby grabs fistfuls of seedless grapes. (8)

2. We barely made it outside on this clear, cloudless day. (10)

3. My mom carefully inspected our bedrooms for neatness. (8)

4. The flatness of our driveway made it useful for playing basketball. (11)

MORE CHALLENGING

5. Julie anticipated that the rubella vaccination would be painless. (9)

6. Cindy made a commitment to volunteer at the homeless shelter every weekend. (12)

7. Seb's willingness to help his classmates instantly made him a candidate for class president. (14)

8. Lance had to take a fitness test to show that he was able to scale the embankment completely on his own. (21)

WORDS

1. Read each word.
2. Underline words that do **not** end with a suffix.
3. Draw a box around words that end with **one** consonant suffix.
4. Circle words that end with **two** consonant suffixes.

agent	carefully	fearful
enjoyment	principal	effortless
speechlessness	locally	thankfulness
payment	address	secretly
helpless	treatment	skillfully

CHALLENGE YOURSELF

1. Find the word that means "having no ability to talk." _____

2. Find the word that tells where you live. _____

3. Find the word that explains how a doctor might help you.

_____

4. Find two words that are jobs.

_____   _____

Reader 1: _____   Date: _____

Reader 2: _____

Reader 3: _____

Words to Preview	Point & Say
1 **published** – printed in a book, a newspaper, a magazine, or online. *She **published** the book of short stories.*	excellent
2 **coyotes** – wild animals that look like small wolves. *The **coyotes** howled at the moon.*	trench
3 **cyclone** – a storm with very strong winds. *The **cyclone** ripped the roof off the house.*	legend
4 **lasso** – a long rope with a loop at one end. *He used the **lasso** to catch the runaway cow.*	

Pecos Bill

Note: Hyphenated words count as one word.

READER 1

Legends say Pecos Bill was the strongest, bravest cowboy of them all.	12
The tall tales about him are like those about the lumberjack Paul Bunyan.	25
Both men do things in their stories that no real person could do.	38

The first stories of this brave cowboy were published in the early 1900s.	51
In these tales, we are told that Pecos Bill was born in Texas in 1832. When	67
he was young, his family moved west. As their wagon rolled along the	80
bumpy road, Pecos Bill fell out, but his parents didn't see him fall. Some	94
coyotes found him and raised him. This is just the beginning of the	107
amazing things that happened to Pecos Bill.	114

READER 2

After the first Pecos Bill stories became popular, many more were written.	126
The stories tell about Pecos Bill being an excellent horseman, but he	138
could ride more than just a horse. He could ride a mountain lion, too.	152
He could even ride a cyclone!	158

Pecos Bill was braver and stronger than any other cowboy. In one tall	171
tale, he fought with a rattlesnake. After he beat the snake, he used it as	186
a lasso to catch bulls. In another tall tale, he dug a trench for a huge	202
river with just a stick.	207

READER 3

Pecos Bill had one true love. That was Slue-Foot Sue. He first saw Sue	221
riding a giant catfish. Soon after, they got married.	230

On their wedding day, Sue tried to ride Pecos Bill's horse, but the horse	244
did not like Sue, so it bounced her off its back. One story says she	259
bounced so high that she landed on the moon. Another story says she	272
kept bouncing back and forth from the ground to the moon. In both	285
stories, Pecos Bill knew he had lost his bride. This made him so sad that	300
he howled at the moon. Legend has it, this is why coyotes still howl at	315
the moon.	317

There are different stories about how Pecos Bill died. Some say he	329
laughed himself to death after seeing a man pretend to be a cowboy	342
with lizard skin boots. No matter how different the tales are, Pecos Bill is	356
always a hero who is larger than life.	364

Calculation Boxes

	Reader 1		Reader 2	Reader 3
		Number of Words at Bracket		
		Subtract: Number of Words at Subhead	-114	-207
Number of Words at Bracket		Equals: Number of Words Attempted		
Subtract: Number of Errors	–	Subtract: Number of Errors	–	–
Equals: Words Correct per Minute (WCPM)		Equals: Words Correct per Minute (WCPM)		
Accuracy Percentage	%	Accuracy Percentage	%	%

Reader 1: _____   Date: _____

Reader 2: _____

Reader 3: _____

Pecos Bill

Note: Hyphenated words count as one word.

READER 1

Legends say Pecos Bill was the strongest, bravest cowboy of them all.	12
The tall tales about him are like those about the lumberjack Paul Bunyan.	25
Both men do things in their stories that no real person could do.	38

The first stories of this brave cowboy were published in the early 1900s.	51
In these tales, we are told that Pecos Bill was born in Texas in 1832. When	67
he was young, his family moved west. As their wagon rolled along the	80
bumpy road, Pecos Bill fell out, but his parents didn't see him fall. Some	94
coyotes found him and raised him. This is just the beginning of the	107
amazing things that happened to Pecos Bill.	114

READER 2

After the first Pecos Bill stories became popular, many more were written.	126
The stories tell about Pecos Bill being an excellent horseman, but he	138
could ride more than just a horse. He could ride a mountain lion, too.	152
He could even ride a cyclone!	158

Pecos Bill was braver and stronger than any other cowboy. In one tall	171
tale, he fought with a rattlesnake. After he beat the snake, he used it as	186
a lasso to catch bulls. In another tall tale, he dug a trench for a huge	202
river with just a stick.	207

READER 3

Pecos Bill had one true love. That was Slue-Foot Sue. He first saw Sue	221
riding a giant catfish. Soon after, they got married.	230

On their wedding day, Sue tried to ride Pecos Bill's horse, but the horse	244
did not like Sue, so it bounced her off its back. One story says she	259
bounced so high that she landed on the moon. Another story says she	272
kept bouncing back and forth from the ground to the moon. In both	285

stories, Pecos Bill knew he had lost his bride. This made him so sad that	300
he howled at the moon. Legend has it, this is why coyotes still howl at	315
the moon.	317

There are different stories about how Pecos Bill died. Some say he	329
laughed himself to death after seeing a man pretend to be a cowboy	342
with lizard skin boots. No matter how different the tales are, Pecos Bill is	356
always a hero who is larger than life.	364

Investigate the Text

1. <u>Underline</u> the sentence that tells **where** and **when** Pecos Bill was born.
   Write ① at the beginning of this underlined sentence.

2. <u>Underline</u> the sentences that tell **what types** of things Pecos Bill rode other than horses.
   Write ② at the beginning of these underlined sentences.

3. <u>Underline</u> the sentences that explain **why** Pecos Bill howled at the moon.
   Write ③ at the beginning of these underlined sentences.

4. <u>Underline</u> the sentence that tells **what** Pecos Bill used as a lasso.
   Write ④ at the beginning of this underlined sentence.

Calculation Boxes

	Reader 1		Reader 2	Reader 3
		Number of Words at Bracket		
		Subtract: Number of Words at Subhead	-114	-207
Number of Words at Bracket		Equals: Number of Words Attempted		
Subtract: Number of Errors	–	Subtract: Number of Errors	–	–
Equals: Words Correct per Minute (WCPM)		Equals: Words Correct per Minute (WCPM)		
Accuracy Percentage	%	Accuracy Percentage	%	%

Mark It!

1. research<u>er</u>
2. dependable
3. shouting
4. poisonous
5. thickest
6. grumpy
7. gardener
8. flexible
9. scratches
10. painter
11. chewy
12. stackable

Read It!

1. thickest	chewy	researcher
2. scratches	grumpy	dependable
3. shouting	poisonous	gardener
4. flexible	painter	stackable
5. dependable	shouting	chewy
6. poisonous	researcher	scratches
7. grumpy	stackable	thickest
8. gardener	flexible	painter

Word Sort

Underline the suffix with one line. Place a checkmark in the correct column.
The *schwa* spellings are circled.

CHALLENGING

Consonant Suffix	Vowel Suffix

1. vis(i)ble
2. reckl(e)ss
3. brighter
4. tricky

MORE CHALLENGING

Consonant Suffix	Vowel Suffix

5. leg(a)lly
6. fearl(e)ss
7. (e)mployer
8. prefix(e)s

MOST CHALLENGING

Consonant Suffix	Vowel Suffix

9. (a)mazem(e)nt
10. c(o)mfort(a)ble
11. forg(ive)n(e)ss
12. hazard(ou)s

CHALLENGING

1. passes the hardest history test (5)
2. smallest dishes go on the top shelf (7)
3. is capable of enjoying the petting zoo (7)
4. had two different viruses at the same time (8)

MORE CHALLENGING

5. editing in pen is acceptable in sixth grade (8)
6. enjoys creamy peanut butter more than chunky (7)
7. the fastest player got the ball past the goalkeeper (9)
8. does crunches, lunges, and jumping jacks in gym class (9)

CHALLENGING

1. Greg is totally believable as a banker or as a preacher. (11)
2. Andrew relaxes on a comfortable hammock in his backyard. (9)
3. On her birthday, Grace wishes for trendy jeans and a tasty lemony dessert. (13)
4. The reporter is informing the public about the pesky pothole along the highway. (13)

MORE CHALLENGING

5. Working outdoors, like gardeners and farmers do, is fulfilling and boosts your physical fitness. (14)
6. The outstanding dressmaker insists on adding sashes and lace to every silky, flowing ball gown. (15)
7. Did the bag containing the cheaper, darker coffee beans make it to the grumpy retailer on time? (17)
8. While sitting in the library, Lucas and Charley were discussing how predictable the closing chapter of their novel was. (19)

1. Read each sentence.
2. <u>Underline</u> all of the vowel suffixes.
3. (Circle) all of the consonant suffixes.
4. Draw a |box| around all of the words that contain **both** a vowel suffix **and** a consonant suffix.

1. Henry was dangerously close to slipping over the edge of the tallest cliff.

2. Can we have a meaningful conversation about the development of better-selling relishes?

3. The amazingly comfortable couch has been broken by the children jumping and dancing on it numerous times.

CHALLENGE YOURSELF

Find base words that could end in two different vowel suffixes, and write the two words on the lines. Example: <u>**deeper**</u> (er)   <u>**deepest**</u> (est)

1. _____ (es)   _____ (ing)

2. _____ (er)   _____ (est)

3. _____ (es)   _____ (y)

4. _____ (able)   _____ (ing)

Come up with your own!

5. _____   _____

6. _____   _____

Reader 1: _____ Date: _____

Reader 2: _____

Reader 3: _____

Words to Preview	Point & Say
1 folktales – stories that are made up and passed along orally by common, everyday people. *My grandpa tells me **folktales** every time I go to visit him.* **2 jack-o'-lantern** – a carved pumpkin with a light inside. *Many houses display a **jack-o'-lantern** on Halloween.* **3 Revolutionary War** – the war in which the American colonists fought for freedom from Great Britain. *The **Revolutionary War** was more than 200 years ago.* **4 Ichabod Crane** – (pronounced Ick-uh-bod Crane) the main character in a famous story called *The Legend of Sleepy Hollow.* *The story does not tell if **Ichabod Crane** was caught by the Headless Horseman.*	legend wealthy

The Headless Horseman

Note: Hyphenated words count as one word.

READER 1

Some dark and windy night, you may meet the Headless Horseman.	11
If you do—watch out!	16
In truth, the Headless Horseman is not real. He is a character in a story	31
called *The Legend of Sleepy Hollow.* A man named Washington Irving	42
wrote the story. He wrote it in 1820, almost 200 years ago. It was one of	58
the first short stories to be published in America. The story was part of a	73
collection, which means it was published with some of Irving's other works.	85
It is one of the oldest American stories that people still enjoy reading.	98

READER 2

The idea for Irving's story might have come from old German folktales.	110
In some of the German tales, the Headless Horseman is a ghost. The	123
ghost rides a dark horse. He blows a horn and waves a sword as he rides.	139
In some tales, the ghost has a jack-o'-lantern for a head.	150

Irving's story takes place in a small town called Sleepy Hollow. The	162
Headless Horseman is the ghost of a soldier from the Revolutionary War.	174
In the story, the soldier's head is taken off by a cannonball in battle. Late	189
each night, the soldier goes out to look for his lost head, and he brings	204
trouble to those he passes on the way.	212

READER 3

Much of Irving's story is about Ichabod Crane, a tall and slender teacher.	225
Crane and another man, Brom Bones, both want to marry the same	237
beautiful and wealthy woman. One fall night, the two men are invited	249
to go to a party at the woman's house. Some of the guests share stories	264
about the Headless Horseman wandering around the country and the	274
graveyard. Late that night, Crane leaves the party long after Brom Bones	286
and everyone else. The Headless Horseman, holding his head on his lap,	298
rides after Crane. The Headless Horseman throws his own head at	309
Crane's head, and Crane is never heard from again. The next day,	321
only Crane's hat and a shattered pumpkin are found.	330

When the story ends, the reader does not know what happened to	342
Ichabod Crane. Was he caught by the Headless Horseman? Did Brom	353
Bones dress up as the Headless Horseman and attack Ichabod Crane?	364
The story doesn't say.	368

The Legend of Sleepy Hollow is now part of American legend. Movies	380
and TV shows are still made about the Headless Horseman. There are	392
even comic books about the famous story.	399

Calculation Boxes	Reader 1		Reader 2	Reader 3
		Number of Words at Bracket		
		Subtract: Number of Words at Subhead	-98	-212
Number of Words at Bracket		Equals: Number of Words Attempted		
Subtract: Number of Errors	–	Subtract: Number of Errors	–	–
Equals: Words Correct per Minute (WCPM)		Equals: Words Correct per Minute (WCPM)		
Accuracy Percentage	%	Accuracy Percentage	%	%

Reader 1: _____   Date: _____

Reader 2: _____

Reader 3: _____

The Headless Horseman

Note: Hyphenated words count as one word.

READER 1

Some dark and windy night, you may meet the Headless Horseman.	11
If you do—watch out!	16

In truth, the Headless Horseman is not real. He is a character in a story	31
called *The Legend of Sleepy Hollow*. A man named Washington Irving	42
wrote the story. He wrote it in 1820, almost 200 years ago. It was one of	58
the first short stories to be published in America. The story was part of a	73
collection, which means it was published with some of Irving's other works.	85
It is one of the oldest American stories that people still enjoy reading.	98

READER 2

The idea for Irving's story might have come from old German folktales.	110
In some of the German tales, the Headless Horseman is a ghost. The	123
ghost rides a dark horse. He blows a horn and waves a sword as he rides.	139
In some tales, the ghost has a jack-o'-lantern for a head.	150

Irving's story takes place in a small town called Sleepy Hollow. The	162
Headless Horseman is the ghost of a soldier from the Revolutionary War.	174
In the story, the soldier's head is taken off by a cannonball in battle. Late	189
each night, the soldier goes out to look for his lost head, and he brings	204
trouble to those he passes on the way.	212

READER 3

Much of Irving's story is about Ichabod Crane, a tall and slender teacher.	225
Crane and another man, Brom Bones, both want to marry the same	237
beautiful and wealthy woman. One fall night, the two men are invited	249
to go to a party at the woman's house. Some of the guests share stories	264
about the Headless Horseman wandering around the country and the	274
graveyard. Late that night, Crane leaves the party long after Brom Bones	286
and everyone else. The Headless Horseman, holding his head on his lap,	298

rides after Crane. The Headless Horseman throws his own head at	309
Crane's head, and Crane is never heard from again. The next day,	321
only Crane's hat and a shattered pumpkin are found.	330

When the story ends, the reader does not know what happened to	342
Ichabod Crane. Was he caught by the Headless Horseman? Did Brom	353
Bones dress up as the Headless Horseman and attack Ichabod Crane?	364
The story doesn't say.	368

The Legend of Sleepy Hollow is now part of American legend. Movies	380
and TV shows are still made about the Headless Horseman. There are	392
even comic books about the famous story.	399

Investigate the Text

1. <u>Underline</u> the sentence that tells **<u>where</u>** the idea for the Headless Horseman may have come from.
   Write ① at the beginning of this underlined sentence.

2. <u>Underline</u> the sentence that tells **<u>how</u>** the Headless Horseman lost his head.
   Write ② at the beginning of this underlined sentence.

3. <u>Underline</u> the sentence that explains **<u>what</u>** was found in the place where Crane went missing.
   Write ③ at the beginning of this underlined sentence.

4. <u>Underline</u> the sentence that explains **<u>why</u>** the Headless Horseman rode around at night.
   Write ④ at the beginning of this underlined sentence.

Calculation Boxes

	Reader 1		Reader 2	Reader 3
		Number of Words at Bracket		
		Subtract: Number of Words at Subhead	-98	-212
Number of Words at Bracket		Equals: Number of Words Attempted		
Subtract: Number of Errors	–	Subtract: Number of Errors	–	–
Equals: Words Correct per Minute (WCPM)		Equals: Words Correct per Minute (WCPM)		
Accuracy Percentage	%	Accuracy Percentage	%	%

Mark It!

1. w i n n e r
2. a p p e a r e d
3. a d m i t t e d
4. g i f t e d
5. o r d e r e d
6. g l a d d e s t
7. r e m i n d e d
8. s c r a t c h e d
9. b e g i n n e r
10. s n a p p y
11. d e l i v e r e d
12. f o r g e t t a b l e

Read It!

1. admitted	snappy	beginner
2. forgettable	ordered	winner
3. gladdest	reminded	appeared
4. scratched	delivered	gifted
5. ordered	appeared	admitted
6. winner	gladdest	reminded
7. delivered	beginner	forgettable
8. gifted	scratched	snappy

Word Sort

Circle the suffix, and underline the base word. Count and circle the number of syllables in the base word. Place a checkmark in the correct column to explain whether or not the suffix adds a syllable. The *schwa* spellings are circled in the base words.

CHALLENGING

	Syllables in Base Word			Suffix Adds a Syllable	Suffix Does Not Add a Syllable
1. detail(ed)	1	(2)	3		✓
2. sloppy	1	2	3		
3. hopper	1	2	3		
4. failed	1	2	3		

MORE CHALLENGING

	Syllables in Base Word			Suffix Adds a Syllable	Suffix Does Not Add a Syllable
5. c(o)mmanded	1	2	3		
6. snipping	1	2	3		
7. itched	1	2	3		
8. flattest	1	2	3		

MOST CHALLENGING

	Syllables in Base Word			Suffix Adds a Syllable	Suffix Does Not Add a Syllable
9. r(e)member´	1	2	3		
10. digested	1	2	3		
11. overcrowded	1	2	3		
12. programming	1	2	3		

CHALLENGING

1. chanted along with the drummer (5)

2. hopping in puddles on the hottest day (7)

3. drew with the sharpest colored pencils (6)

4. grasped the ropes of the thinner swing (7)

MORE CHALLENGING

5. ate grilled red snapper in an overcrowded diner (8)

6. pretended to be puzzled by the messy bedroom (8)

7. regretted swimming and diving right after eating (7)

8. gulped carbonated lemonade on the sunny day (7)

CHALLENGING

1. The cake topping was crushed chocolate cookies. (7)

2. Sledding is an exciting winter activity when you are bored. (10)

3. Zack's mommy and daddy planned a surprise party for him. (10)

4. My melted ice cream began dripping down my arm and onto my faded dress. (14)

MORE CHALLENGING

5. The stuffed teddy bear seemed more huggable when Grayson was not well rested. (13)

6. Spectators drenched the fastest runners as they passed by the curved stairway. (12)

7. Trimming the branches and splitting the stumps with the ax was more difficult than I expected. (16)

8. The winner quickly stretched after the game and then dropped his sloppy, muddy sneakers and jacket by the back door. (20)

Circle **yes** or **no** for each question. Write the base word with the suffix on the line.

Is the last syllable a 1-1-1 syllable?		Is this a vowel suffix?		Should I double the final consonant?	Write the word.
cost	Y or Ⓝ	ing	Ⓨ or N	Y or Ⓝ	**costing**
grab	Y or N	ed	Y or N	Y or N	
drop	Y or N	ing	Y or N	Y or N	
cancel	Y or N	s	Y or N	Y or N	
ship	Y or N	ing	Y or N	Y or N	
luck	Y or N	y	Y or N	Y or N	
begin	Y or N	ing	Y or N	Y or N	
forget	Y or N	ful	Y or N	Y or N	
weak	Y or N	ness	Y or N	Y or N	

CHALLENGE YOURSELF

Underline the base word. Write **syllable** or **sound** on the line to show whether *suffix* **-ed** adds a syllable or a sound to the base word.

1. gulped _____

2. existed _____

3. yelled _____

4. snatched _____

5. filmed _____

6. insisted _____

7. responded _____

8. blinked _____

9. talented _____

10. attached _____

11. risked _____

12. leveled _____

Reader 1: _____ Date: _____

Reader 2: _____

Reader 3: _____

Words to Preview	Point & Say
1 **exaggerated** – based on truth, but made greater or larger. _Legends are often **exaggerated** stories about the lives of real people._	Illinois
2 **Massachusetts** – a state in the northeastern part of the United States. _Some of the colonists from England moved to **Massachusetts**._	Indiana
3 **nurseries** – places where plants are grown to be sold. _Every spring we visit several local **nurseries** to buy flowers for our garden._	Ohio
4 **settlers** – people who establish a colony in a new area. _The **settlers** decided to build their house by the river._	

Johnny Appleseed

Note: Hyphenated words count as one word.

READER 1

The story of Johnny Appleseed is more than a legend. Johnny	11
Appleseed really did plant many apple seeds. The stories about	21
Johnny Appleseed may be exaggerated, but they are most likely	31
based on truth.	34

Johnny Appleseed's real name was John Chapman. He earned the	44
nickname Johnny Appleseed when he was an adult. He was an unusual	56
person. One unusual thing about Johnny was the way he dressed. He	68
wore old, torn clothes, and he never wore shoes. Some say he used a	82
coffee sack as a shirt.	87

READER 2

John Chapman was born in Massachusetts in 1774. While growing up,	98
he learned to plant and care for apple trees. As a young man, he	112
left Massachusetts and headed west. Each place he went, he started	123
nurseries so settlers would have trees. Many of the seeds Chapman	134
planted were for apple trees.	139

John first started nurseries in Pennsylvania, and then he moved to Ohio.	151
He also had nurseries in Indiana and Illinois. He planted more apple	163
seeds in Ohio than anywhere else. Not long after he started planting	175
apple seeds, people began calling him Johnny Appleseed.	183

READER 3

Some stories about Johnny say he scattered seeds wherever he went.	194
However, he did not scatter seeds without any thought. He carefully	205
planned where he would plant his nurseries, and he planted the seeds in	218
neat rows. He found land in areas that had not been settled yet.	231
After he planted seeds in one place, Johnny Appleseed would go to	243
new places and start more nurseries. In a year or two, he would return to	258
the nurseries where new trees were growing. He would sell the new trees	271
to the settlers. The settlers dug up the trees and planted them on their	285
own land.	287
Johnny Appleseed was a kind and fair businessman. If people did not	299
have money to buy the trees, Johnny traded the trees for other things.	312
Sometimes, he gave trees to people who couldn't afford them. He felt it	325
was more important for others to have apple trees than it was for him to	340
have money. He wanted to plant enough apple trees to make sure no	353
one ever went hungry.	357
Johnny Appleseed lived a simple life. He was a kind man who helped	370
other people whenever he could. He was good to animals. He never	382
owned a home, and he often slept outside as he traveled. Sometimes	394
people would invite him to sleep in their homes. People were happy to	407
welcome such a kind man into their homes.	415

Calculation Boxes

	Reader 1		Reader 2	Reader 3
		Number of Words at Bracket		
		Subtract: Number of Words at Subhead	-87	-183
Number of Words at Bracket		Equals: Number of Words Attempted		
Subtract: Number of Errors	–	Subtract: Number of Errors	–	–
Equals: Words Correct per Minute (WCPM)		Equals: Words Correct per Minute (WCPM)		
Accuracy Percentage	%	Accuracy Percentage	%	%

Reader 1: _____   Date: _____

Reader 2: _____

Reader 3: _____

Johnny Appleseed

Note: Hyphenated words count as one word.

READER 1

The story of Johnny Appleseed is more than a legend. Johnny	11
Appleseed really did plant many apple seeds. The stories about	21
Johnny Appleseed may be exaggerated, but they are most likely	31
based on truth.	34

Johnny Appleseed's real name was John Chapman. He earned the	44
nickname Johnny Appleseed when he was an adult. He was an unusual	56
person. One unusual thing about Johnny was the way he dressed. He	68
wore old, torn clothes, and he never wore shoes. Some say he used a	82
coffee sack as a shirt.	87

READER 2

John Chapman was born in Massachusetts in 1774. While growing up,	98
he learned to plant and care for apple trees. As a young man, he	112
left Massachusetts and headed west. Each place he went, he started	123
nurseries so settlers would have trees. Many of the seeds Chapman	134
planted were for apple trees.	139

John first started nurseries in Pennsylvania, and then he moved to Ohio.	151
He also had nurseries in Indiana and Illinois. He planted more apple	163
seeds in Ohio than anywhere else. Not long after he started planting	175
apple seeds, people began calling him Johnny Appleseed.	183

READER 3

Some stories about Johnny say he scattered seeds wherever he went.	194
However, he did not scatter seeds without any thought. He carefully	205
planned where he would plant his nurseries, and he planted the seeds in	218
neat rows. He found land in areas that had not been settled yet.	231

After he planted seeds in one place, Johnny Appleseed would go to	243
new places and start more nurseries. In a year or two, he would return to	258
the nurseries where new trees were growing. He would sell the new trees	271

to the settlers. The settlers dug up the trees and planted them on their	285
own land.	287

Johnny Appleseed was a kind and fair businessman. If people did not	299
have money to buy the trees, Johnny traded the trees for other things.	312
Sometimes, he gave trees to people who couldn't afford them. He felt it	325
was more important for others to have apple trees than it was for him to	340
have money. He wanted to plant enough apple trees to make sure no	353
one ever went hungry.	357

Johnny Appleseed lived a simple life. He was a kind man who helped	370
other people whenever he could. He was good to animals. He never	382
owned a home, and he often slept outside as he traveled. Sometimes	394
people would invite him to sleep in their homes. People were happy to	407
welcome such a kind man into their homes.	415

Investigate the Text

1. Underline the sentence that gives Johnny Appleseed's real name.
   Write ① at the beginning of this underlined sentence.

2. Underline the sentences that describe **how** Johnny Appleseed dressed.
   Write ② at the beginning of these underlined sentences.

3. Underline the sentence that explains **what** Johnny Appleseed thought was more important than having money.
   Write ③ at the beginning of this underlined sentence.

4. Underline the sentence that tells **when** Johnny Appleseed would return to the new trees growing in his nurseries.
   Write ④ at the beginning of this underlined sentence.

Calculation Boxes

	Reader 1		Reader 2	Reader 3
		Number of Words at Bracket		
		Subtract: Number of Words at Subhead	-87	-183
Number of Words at Bracket		Equals: Number of Words Attempted		
Subtract: Number of Errors	–	Subtract: Number of Errors	–	–
Equals: Words Correct per Minute (WCPM)		Equals: Words Correct per Minute (WCPM)		
Accuracy Percentage	%	Accuracy Percentage	%	%

Mark It!

1. <u>un</u>even
2. discolor
3. impact
4. confirm
5. inspire
6. disorder
7. conserve
8. immature
9. unbroken
10. disagree
11. incomplete
12. impolite

Read It!

1. confirm
2. disagree
3. inspire
4. immature
5. impolite
6. conserve
7. unbroken
8. impact

impact
unbroken
disorder
conserve
confirm
uneven
incomplete
discolor

incomplete
impolite
uneven
discolor
disorder
inspire
disagree
immature

Separate each word into the prefix and the base or root word. The *schwa* spellings are circled.

CHALLENGING

1. install
2. discard
3. unfair
4. impress

Prefix	Base or Root Word
in	**stall**

MORE CHALLENGING

5. invent
6. unclear
7. disown
8. concert

Prefix	Base or Root Word

MOST CHALLENGING

9. uncomm⊙n
10. inc⊙rrect
11. dis⊕ngage
12. cons⊕quence

Prefix	Base or Root Word

CHALLENGING

1. concert will impress and inspire (5)
2. can impeach the new president (5)
3. should invite the children indoors (5)
4. has to disarm the constant door alarm (7)

MORE CHALLENGING

5. cannot imagine how animal instinct works (6)
6. must disinfect the glass trophy display case (7)
7. insist on a respectful attitude in the classroom (8)
8. should not interrupt the informational meeting (6)

CHALLENGING

1. Kate will try to invent a way to unlock any door in an emergency. (14)
2. It is impolite to imply that my dog would inflict harm on the mailman. (14)
3. If you have a question about the concert, you can inquire at the help desk. (15)
4. The contents of the discolored tote bag included important papers and the missing keys. (14)

MORE CHALLENGING

5. If you want to improve your grades, you should ask your teacher to explain any unclear concepts. (17)
6. I get the impression that the competition will be difficult, but I am convinced that you are prepared. (18)
7. Hunter has confidence that he can dispel the rumor that he cheated with notes hidden inside his desk. (18)
8. The early birthday party was an unexpected and incredible surprise, and I was completely unaware that it was going to happen. (21)

Word Creation

Add a prefix to each word part to create a real word. Words with two lines have two prefixes that can be added.

Prefixes

dis-   con-   in-
un-   im-

Base/Root Words	New Real Words	
1 possible	_impossible_	
2 struct	_____	_____
3 like	_____	_____
4 agree	_____	
5 side	_____	
6 vent	_____	_____
7 mature	_____	
8 text	_____	
9 tent	_____	_____
10 card	_____	
11 pact	_____	

CHALLENGE YOURSELF

Choose the correct prefix so that each sentence makes sense.

1. The teacher will (con/in) _____struct the students to read three chapters.

2. Please remember to (dis/un) _____able the alarm when you enter.

3. My mom (con/in) _____sists that I do my homework before dinner.

4. The nuns had to return to the (con/in) _____vent before dusk.

5. (Dis/Un) _____like humans, sharks' skeletons are made only of cartilage.

Reader 1: _____   Date: _____

Reader 2: _____

Reader 3: _____

Words to Preview	Point & Say
① Montgomery – a large city in Alabama. _Montgomery is the capital of Alabama._	Tuskegee courage
② seamstress – a woman who earns a living by sewing. _Which **seamstress** made that beautiful wedding dress?_	
③ segregation – the act of separating people by race. _Segregation in the South did not allow black and white children to go to the same schools._	
④ protested – took action in order to express disagreement about something. _Many people **protested** the high price of gas by riding their bikes to work._	
⑤ boycott – a refusal to buy, sell, or use something. _We joined the grape **boycott** and did not buy grapes._	

Rosa Parks

Note: Hyphenated words count as one word.

READER 1

After a long day at work, a black woman took a seat on the bus. The bus	17
began to fill with riders.	22
A few stops later, a white man stepped on, but there were no seats left.	37
The bus driver went to the middle of the bus, and he asked the black	52
woman to stand up so the white man could have her seat. She refused.	66
The bus driver called the police, and they arrested the woman for	78
breaking the law.	81
The date was December 1, 1955. The place was Montgomery, Alabama.	92
The woman was Rosa Parks.	97
Rosa Parks was a seamstress, but she became an American hero that	109
day. Her actions, and the actions of many others, triggered huge	120
changes for blacks in the United States.	127

READER 2

Rosa Parks was born in 1913 in Tuskegee, Alabama. She moved to	139
Montgomery when she was young. She grew up when segregation was	150

legal in many parts of the United States. In Alabama and many other	163
states, blacks and whites went to different schools. Black people could	174
work at most restaurants, but many of the restaurants where blacks	185
worked only served food to whites.	191

Most of the people riding buses in Montgomery were black. In 1900, the	204
city passed laws with strict rules for seating on buses. Black people had to	218
sit in the middle or the back of buses, and only white people could use the	234
front. A black person could not sit across from a white person. If the bus	249
was full, black people had to give their seats to white people.	261

READER 3

Rosa was 42 when she refused to give her seat on the bus to a white man.	278
That decision took a lot of courage. She knew she would be arrested.	291

Four days after Rosa's arrest, blacks in the city protested. They began	303
a boycott of the buses. For more than a year, the black people in	317
Montgomery stayed off the buses even if that meant they had to ride	330
their bikes or walk as many as 12 miles to work. Some whites joined the	345
boycott to show their support. The bus companies made a lot less money	358
during the boycott because so many people quit riding the buses.	369

Finally, in 1956, the law changed. Blacks could sit wherever they wanted	381
on the bus, and they started riding the buses again.	391

Rosa Parks had worked for equal rights for blacks in America even before	404
her arrest. After her arrest and the boycott of the buses, she was a famous	419
woman. She continued her work toward equal rights the rest of her life.	432

Rosa was 92 when she died. She is fondly remembered for her courage.	445
She is a hero who brought about a better life in America.	457

Calculation Boxes

	Reader 1		Reader 2	Reader 3
		Number of Words at Bracket		
Number of Words at Bracket		Subtract: Number of Words at Subhead	-127	-261
		Equals: Number of Words Attempted		
Subtract: Number of Errors	−	Subtract: Number of Errors	−	−
Equals: Words Correct per Minute (WCPM)		Equals: Words Correct per Minute (WCPM)		
Accuracy Percentage	%	Accuracy Percentage	%	%

Reader 1: _____   Date: _____

Reader 2: _____

Reader 3: _____

Rosa Parks

Note: Hyphenated words count as one word.

READER 1

After a long day at work, a black woman took a seat on the bus. The bus	17
began to fill with riders.	22
A few stops later, a white man stepped on, but there were no seats left.	37
The bus driver went to the middle of the bus, and he asked the black	52
woman to stand up so the white man could have her seat. She refused.	66
The bus driver called the police, and they arrested the woman for	78
breaking the law.	81
The date was December 1, 1955. The place was Montgomery, Alabama.	92
The woman was Rosa Parks.	97
Rosa Parks was a seamstress, but she became an American hero that	109
day. Her actions, and the actions of many others, triggered huge	120
changes for blacks in the United States.	127

READER 2

Rosa Parks was born in 1913 in Tuskegee, Alabama. She moved to	139
Montgomery when she was young. She grew up when segregation was	150
legal in many parts of the United States. In Alabama and many other	163
states, blacks and whites went to different schools. Black people could	174
work at most restaurants, but many of the restaurants where blacks	185
worked only served food to whites.	191
Most of the people riding buses in Montgomery were black. In 1900, the	204
city passed laws with strict rules for seating on buses. Black people had to	218
sit in the middle or the back of buses, and only white people could use the	234
front. A black person could not sit across from a white person. If the bus	249
was full, black people had to give their seats to white people.	261

READER 3

Rosa was 42 when she refused to give her seat on the bus to a white man.	278
That decision took a lot of courage. She knew she would be arrested.	291

Four days after Rosa's arrest, blacks in the city protested. They began	303
a boycott of the buses. For more than a year, the black people in	317
Montgomery stayed off the buses even if that meant they had to ride	330
their bikes or walk as many as 12 miles to work. Some whites joined the	345
boycott to show their support. The bus companies made a lot less money	358
during the boycott because so many people quit riding the buses.	369
Finally, in 1956, the law changed. Blacks could sit wherever they wanted	381
on the bus, and they started riding the buses again.	391
Rosa Parks had worked for equal rights for blacks in America even before	404
her arrest. After her arrest and the boycott of the buses, she was a famous	419
woman. She continued her work toward equal rights the rest of her life.	432
Rosa was 92 when she died. She is fondly remembered for her courage.	445
She is a hero who brought about a better life in America.	457

Investigate the Text

1 Underline the sentence that tells **what** job Rosa Parks had before the bus boycott.
Write ① at the beginning of this underlined sentence.

2 Underline the sentence that tells **when** Montgomery first passed laws about where blacks had to sit on buses.
Write ② at the beginning of this underlined sentence.

3 Underline the sentence that tells **what** people did to protest Rosa's arrest.
Write ③ at the beginning of this underlined sentence.

4 Underline the sentence that tells **when** Rosa Parks became famous.
Write ④ at the beginning of this underlined sentence.

Calculation Boxes

	Reader 1		Reader 2	Reader 3
Number of Words at Bracket		Number of Words at Bracket		
		Subtract: Number of Words at Subhead	-127	-261
		Equals: Number of Words Attempted		
Number of Words at Bracket				
Subtract: Number of Errors	–	Subtract: Number of Errors	–	–
Equals: Words Correct per Minute (WCPM)		Equals: Words Correct per Minute (WCPM)		
Accuracy Percentage	%	Accuracy Percentage	%	%

Mark It!

1. p r o t e c t
2. p r e s c r i b e
3. r e p e a t
4. p r o g r a m
5. p r e s e n t
6. p r o v i d e

7. r e d u c e
8. p r o h i b i t
9. p r o p e l
10. r e l o c a t e
11. p r e t e n d
12. p r e v e n t i o n

Read It!

1. relocate   provide   present
2. propel   prevention   protect
3. prescribe   prohibit   repeat
4. reduce   pretend   program
5. protect   prescribe   prohibit
6. repeat   propel   prevention
7. pretend   present   reduce
8. provide   program   relocate

Word Sort

Separate each word into the prefix and the base or root word. The *schwa* spellings are circled.

CHALLENGING

1. recharge
2. pr**o**vide
3. pr**e**fer
4. r**e**call

Prefix	Base or Root Word
re	charge

MORE CHALLENGING

5. pr**o**duce
6. remod**e**l
7. pr**e**serve
8. r**e**quest

Prefix	Base or Root Word

MOST CHALLENGING

9. pr**o**fess
10. pr**e**sent
11. protractor
12. recopy

Prefix	Base or Root Word

CHALLENGING

1. make a prediction before reading (5)

2. will return and provide potato salad (6)

3. prefers to retire at the end of the year (9)

4. needs to prepare a report on pandas (7)

MORE CHALLENGING

5. prefers to be protective of her little sister (8)

6. not able to recycle foam at the present time (9)

7. can prohibit him from giving a pretest in math (9)

8. should proceed to the revolving door in the hotel (9)

CHALLENGING

1. I prefer to grow my own garlic plants by replanting cloves. (11)

2. The students in the music program produce a concert every winter. (11)

3. Harrison cannot recall if he recorded notes during our conversation. (10)

4. If you send in the rebate, the company will repay some of your cash. (14)

MORE CHALLENGING

5. Pamela gave a presentation based on her report on the reflective properties of tinfoil. (14)

6. We should let the professional contractors take care of that basement remodeling job. (13)

7. Some illnesses are preventable if you take protective steps like cleaning your hands regularly. (14)

8. My family had to relocate to a new city because of my dad's new management position. (16)

▶ Word Creation

Add prefixes, suffixes, or both to create new words.

Prefixes

dis-	im-	pre-
con-	in-	pro-
un-	re-	

Suffixes

-s	-ness	-es	-est
-ful	-ment	-y	-able
-ly	-ous	-ing	-ible
-less	-ed	-er	

Words   New Real Words

1. play   <u>playful</u>   _____   _____
2. fresh   _____   _____   _____
3. help   _____   _____   _____
4. thank   _____   _____   _____
5. tend   _____   _____   _____
6. cord   _____   _____   _____
7. gram   _____   _____   _____
8. print   _____   _____   _____
9. joy   _____   _____   _____
10. trust   _____   _____   _____

CHALLENGE YOURSELF

Using the base/root words below and the combinations of prefixes and suffixes listed below the lines, fill in the blanks to create real words. If you cannot think of a real word, you may create a nonsense word.*

1. _____ grate _____ _____
   prefix   suffix   suffix

2. _____ _____ duce
   prefix   prefix

3. _____ place _____ _____
   prefix   suffix   suffix

4. _____ _____ nect
   prefix   prefix

*If a word you create happens to be a nonsense word, be prepared to explain and defend it.

Reader 1: _____   Date: _____

Reader 2: _____

Reader 3: _____

Words to Preview	Point & Say
1 **aviator** – a person who flies airplanes; a pilot. _He was the first **aviator** to fly an airplane across the ocean._	license
2 **vanished** – disappeared completely from sight. _The moon **vanished** behind the clouds._	
3 **merry-go-round** – a ride at a fair with a round platform that spins and has seats in the form of horses or other animals. _I like to ride the outside horse on the **merry-go-round**._	
4 **biplane** – an airplane with two main wings stacked one above the other. _Pilots stopped flying **biplanes** by the end of the 1930s._	

Amelia Earhart

Note: Hyphenated words count as one word.

READER 1

Amelia Earhart was a famous aviator. She set many records for flying, but	13
her last trip was a failure. She tried to fly around the world. She flew almost	29
the whole way before her plane vanished over the Pacific Ocean.	40
Amelia Earhart was born in 1897. She first saw an airplane at a state fair	55
when she was ten years old. Her father asked her if she wanted to take a	71
flight, but she said no because she wanted to ride on the merry-go-round.	84
In 1920, Earhart went to an air show with her father. At the air show, she	100
took her first ride in an airplane. As soon as the plane got off the ground,	116
Amelia knew she wanted to learn to fly.	124

READER 2

Her dream soon became a reality. A few weeks after her first airplane	137
ride, Earhart took her first flying lesson. Six months later, she bought her	150
first airplane, a bright yellow biplane. In 1923, Earhart became the 16th	162
woman to earn a pilot's license.	168
In 1928, Earhart was invited to fly across the Atlantic Ocean, but only as	182
a passenger. Two men would be the pilots of the plane. Amelia's only	195

job was to keep the flight log. She accepted the invitation, and this flight 209
changed her life. The flight took 20 hours and 40 minutes. When she 222
arrived in England, people were waiting to greet her. Amelia was famous; 234
she was the first woman to cross the Atlantic in a plane. 246

Earhart soon began setting records of her own. Some of her records 258
were for speed, some were for distance, and some were for flying higher 271
than anyone else. 274

READER 3

In 1932, Earhart turned 35 years old. She set one of her most important 288
records that year by being the first woman to fly solo across the Atlantic. 302
It was the longest nonstop flight flown by a woman. Her solo flight took 316
only 14 hours and 56 minutes, which was even faster than her first trip 330
across the Atlantic in 1928. 335

Amelia Earhart planned a trip to fly around the world in 1937. Fred 348
Noonan, her crew member, had the job of charting the flight. Earhart 360
and Noonan started their adventure on May 21, flying from California to 372
Florida. They left Florida on June 1 and made many stops as they flew 386
around the world. 389

Just a month after it left Florida, the plane vanished over the South 402
Pacific. It was last seen on July 2, 1937. Earhart and Noonan had flown 416
almost 22,000 miles and only had about 7,000 miles before their trip 428
would have ended. 431

People searched the sea for weeks. Earhart and Noonan were never 442
found, and neither was the plane, but Earhart is still remembered and 454
will continue to inspire girls and women to follow their dreams. 465

Calculation Boxes	Reader 1		Reader 2	Reader 3
		Number of Words at Bracket		
		Subtract: Number of Words at Subhead	-124	-274
Number of Words at Bracket		Equals: Number of Words Attempted		
Subtract: Number of Errors	–	Subtract: Number of Errors	–	–
Equals: Words Correct per Minute (WCPM)		Equals: Words Correct per Minute (WCPM)		
Accuracy Percentage	%	Accuracy Percentage	%	%

Reader 1: _____   Date: _____

Reader 2: _____

Reader 3: _____

Amelia Earhart

Note: Hyphenated words count as one word.

READER 1

Amelia Earhart was a famous aviator. She set many records for flying, but	13
her last trip was a failure. She tried to fly around the world. She flew almost	29
the whole way before her plane vanished over the Pacific Ocean.	40
Amelia Earhart was born in 1897. She first saw an airplane at a state fair	55
when she was ten years old. Her father asked her if she wanted to take a	71
flight, but she said no because she wanted to ride on the merry-go-round.	84
In 1920, Earhart went to an air show with her father. At the air show, she	100
took her first ride in an airplane. As soon as the plane got off the ground,	116
Amelia knew she wanted to learn to fly.	124

READER 2

Her dream soon became a reality. A few weeks after her first airplane	137
ride, Earhart took her first flying lesson. Six months later, she bought her	150
first airplane, a bright yellow biplane. In 1923, Earhart became the 16th	162
woman to earn a pilot's license.	168
In 1928, Earhart was invited to fly across the Atlantic Ocean, but only as	182
a passenger. Two men would be the pilots of the plane. Amelia's only	195
job was to keep the flight log. She accepted the invitation, and this flight	209
changed her life. The flight took 20 hours and 40 minutes. When she	222
arrived in England, people were waiting to greet her. Amelia was famous;	234
she was the first woman to cross the Atlantic in a plane.	246
Earhart soon began setting records of her own. Some of her records	258
were for speed, some were for distance, and some were for flying higher	271
than anyone else.	274

READER 3

In 1932, Earhart turned 35 years old. She set one of her most important	288
records that year by being the first woman to fly solo across the Atlantic.	302
It was the longest nonstop flight flown by a woman. Her solo flight took	316

only 14 hours and 56 minutes, which was even faster than her first trip	330
across the Atlantic in 1928.	335
Amelia Earhart planned a trip to fly around the world in 1937. Fred	348
Noonan, her crew member, had the job of charting the flight. Earhart	360
and Noonan started their adventure on May 21, flying from California to	372
Florida. They left Florida on June 1 and made many stops as they flew	386
around the world.	389
Just a month after it left Florida, the plane vanished over the South	402
Pacific. It was last seen on July 2, 1937. Earhart and Noonan had flown	416
almost 22,000 miles and only had about 7,000 miles before their trip	428
would have ended.	431
People searched the sea for weeks. Earhart and Noonan were never	442
found, and neither was the plane, but Earhart is still remembered and	454
will continue to inspire girls and women to follow their dreams.	465

Investigate the Text

1. Underline the sentence that tells **where** Amelia Earhart's plane vanished.
   Write ① at the beginning of this underlined sentence.

2. Underline the sentences that tell **when** Earhart first rode in an airplane.
   Write ② at the beginning of these underlined sentences.

3. Underline the sentence that tells **how long** Earhart's solo flight over the Atlantic took.
   Write ③ at the beginning of this underlined sentence.

4. Underline the sentence that tells **how old** Earhart was when she broke the record for longest nonstop flight flown by a woman.
   Write ④ at the beginning of this underlined sentence.

Calculation Boxes

	Reader 1		Reader 2	Reader 3
		Number of Words at Bracket		
		Subtract: Number of Words at Subhead	-124	-274
Number of Words at Bracket		Equals: Number of Words Attempted		
Subtract: Number of Errors	−	Subtract: Number of Errors	−	−
Equals: Words Correct per Minute (WCPM)		Equals: Words Correct per Minute (WCPM)		
Accuracy Percentage	%	Accuracy Percentage	%	%

Mark It!

1. <u>un</u>grate<u>ful</u>
2. conflicting
3. disorderly
4. unwilling
5. preferable
6. constructed
7. impoliteness
8. revolving
9. prolonged
10. disagreement
11. invented
12. unevenly

Read It!

1. prolonged — ungrateful — impoliteness
2. disagreement — preferable — conflicting
3. constructed — unevenly — unwilling
4. revolving — invented — disorderly
5. preferable — unwilling — prolonged
6. impoliteness — revolving — disagreement
7. invented — conflicting — ungrateful
8. unevenly — disorderly — constructed

Separate each word into the prefix, the base or root word, and the suffix. The *schwa* spellings are circled.

CHALLENGING

1. r(e)peat(e)d
2. impairm(e)nt
3. unsafely
4. disowned

Prefix	Base/Root Word	Suffix
re	**peat**	**ed**

MORE CHALLENGING

5. retailer
6. incred(i)ble
7. r(e)spectf(u)l
8. ind(i)rectly

Prefix	Base/Root Word	Suffix

MOST CHALLENGING

9. pr(o)tect(e)d
10. pretreatm(e)nt
11. r(e)fresh(e)s
12. increasing

Prefix	Base/Root Word	Suffix

CHALLENGING

1. made him uneasy and nervous (5)
2. moon reflected in the peaceful water (6)
3. disputed paint colors for the living room (7)
4. was a reminder of her uncommon talent (7)

MORE CHALLENGING

5. will unpack and relocate the picture frames (7)
6. gets to prepare a feast for the reading professor (9)
7. repeated the gorilla impression for all of the fans (9)
8. with orange preserves and chunky peanut butter (7)

CHALLENGING

1. The newly released computer game included a poster. (8)
2. Recently, we held a retirement party at the remodeled factory. (10)
3. The instant replay clearly showed that the running back was illegally tackled. (12)
4. Clair's grandmother was discharged from the hospital with normal test results. (11)

MORE CHALLENGING

5. Grant intended to perform a remarkable concert with his preowned instrument. (11)
6. The small baby quickly rejected the blended peas that were hidden inside the applesauce. (14)
7. Wearing black jeans became unpopular when teens became more interested in brightly colored pants. (14)
8. My puppy is unwilling to eat her crunchy food, so we have to discard all of it and refill her dish with soft, chewable meat and grains. (27)

Add prefixes, endings/suffixes, or both to create as many new real words as you can. Each word you create must include the base word **struct**. You may add more than one prefix or suffix to a word. (Example: de + con + struct + ed = deconstructed)

Beginnings	**Base Word**	**Endings/Suffixes**	
con	struct	ive	al
in		ion	ture
de		ure	ness
re		ed	ly
un		ing	

2-Syllable Words	**3-Syllable Words**	**4-Syllable Words**
		deconstructed
_____	_____	_____
_____	_____	_____
_____	_____	_____
_____	_____	_____
_____	_____	_____
_____	_____	_____
_____	_____	_____
_____	_____	_____
_____	_____	_____
_____	_____	_____

CHALLENGE YOURSELF

Choose **two** words from above, and write **one** sentence that includes both of those words on the lines below.

_____

_____

Reader 1: _____ Date: _____

Reader 2: _____

Reader 3: _____

Words to Preview **Point & Say**

① **surveyor** – a person who gathers information about an area and makes maps.
Before Tammy buys land, she will hire a **surveyor** to make sure she can build there.

② **colonists** – the people who lived in a colony.
The **colonists** in the British colonies had to live by the rules of the king.

③ **plantation** – a large piece of land where one type of crop is tended by workers who live on the land. Before the Civil War, many slaves lived and worked on plantations.
John worked on a coffee **plantation** in Costa Rica for nine years.

colony/ colonies

hurdles

Potomac River

elected

George Washington

Note: Hyphenated words count as one word.

READER 1

George Washington was the first president of the United States of	11
America. He lived more than 200 years ago.	19
Washington was born in 1732 in the colony of Virginia. The king of	32
England ruled the colonies of America when Washington was born.	42
People living in the colonies had to obey the king. He had many laws	56
that the colonists did not agree with though.	64
Washington grew up on a plantation where he often helped plant and	76
harvest the crops. When he was young, he went to school where he	89
learned to read and write. He also learned how to make maps. George	102
Washington used his map-making skills to become a surveyor at about	113
age 17. Washington is given credit for 199 survey maps. About 75 of those	127
maps still exist.	130

READER 2

Young George loved horses, and he took good care of the horses on his	144

family's plantation. Every day, he fed the horses, brushed them, gave	155
them water, and rode them. George was an excellent horseman. He	166
loved riding a horse that would gallop fast and jump high hurdles.	178

At age 27, George Washington married a wealthy young woman named	189
Martha Custis. George and Martha lived on a plantation called Mount	200
Vernon near the Potomac River. Today, Mount Vernon is open to visitors	212
who are interested in seeing where Washington lived.	220

READER 3

Throughout Washington's early career, the colonists continued to disagree	229
with the rules that the king of England made them follow. The colonists	242
decided to go to war against England. They wanted to be free from the	256
king because the colonists did not feel that he treated them fairly. They	269
wanted to be free to rule themselves and create their own laws.	281

By then, Washington was known as a good man and a strong leader	294
in his fight against the British. He was chosen as head of the army.	308
As general, Washington led the soldiers into battle against the king's	319
soldiers. After the colonists won the war, Washington was elected to be	331
the first president of the United States of America.	340

The American people still respect George Washington. He is often called	350
the "Father of our Country." Most people agree that he was a great	364
president. Many places are named after Washington to honor him. One	375
of those places is America's capital city, Washington, DC. Washington's	385
face is also honored on our currency. His face is on the quarter and the	400
one dollar bill.	403

Calculation Boxes	Reader 1		Reader 2	Reader 3
		Number of Words at Bracket		
		Subtract: Number of Words at Subhead	-130	-220
Number of Words at Bracket		Equals: Number of Words Attempted		
Subtract: Number of Errors	−	Subtract: Number of Errors	−	−
Equals: Words Correct per Minute (WCPM)		Equals: Words Correct per Minute (WCPM)		
Accuracy Percentage	%	Accuracy Percentage	%	%

Reader 1: _____ Date: _____

Reader 2: _____

Reader 3: _____

George Washington

Note: Hyphenated words count as one word.

READER 1

George Washington was the first president of the United States of	11
America. He lived more than 200 years ago.	19
Washington was born in 1732 in the colony of Virginia. The king of	32
England ruled the colonies of America when Washington was born.	42
People living in the colonies had to obey the king. He had many laws	56
that the colonists did not agree with though.	64
Washington grew up on a plantation where he often helped plant and	76
harvest the crops. When he was young, he went to school where he	89
learned to read and write. He also learned how to make maps. George	102
Washington used his map-making skills to become a surveyor at about	113
age 17. Washington is given credit for 199 survey maps. About 75 of those	127
maps still exist.	130

READER 2

Young George loved horses, and he took good care of the horses on his	144
family's plantation. Every day, he fed the horses, brushed them, gave	155
them water, and rode them. George was an excellent horseman. He	166
loved riding a horse that would gallop fast and jump high hurdles.	178
At age 27, George Washington married a wealthy young woman named	189
Martha Custis. George and Martha lived on a plantation called Mount	200
Vernon near the Potomac River. Today, Mount Vernon is open to visitors	212
who are interested in seeing where Washington lived.	220

READER 3

Throughout Washington's early career, the colonists continued to disagree	229
with the rules that the king of England made them follow. The colonists	242
decided to go to war against England. They wanted to be free from the	256

king because the colonists did not feel that he treated them fairly. They	269
wanted to be free to rule themselves and create their own laws.	281

By then, Washington was known as a good man and a strong leader	294
in his fight against the British. He was chosen as head of the army.	308
As general, Washington led the soldiers into battle against the king's	319
soldiers. After the colonists won the war, Washington was elected to be	331
the first president of the United States of America.	340

The American people still respect George Washington. He is often called	350
the "Father of our Country." Most people agree that he was a great	364
president. Many places are named after Washington to honor him. One	375
of those places is America's capital city, Washington, DC. Washington's	385
face is also honored on our currency. His face is on the quarter and the	400
one dollar bill.	403

Investigate the Text

1. Underline the sentence that tells **where** Washington was born.
   Write ① at the beginning of this underlined sentence.

2. Underline the sentence that tells **how many** maps Washington made.
   Write ② at the beginning of this underlined sentence.

3. Underline the sentences that explain **why** the colonists went to war against England.
   Write ③ at the beginning of these underlined sentences.

4. Underline the sentence that tells the name of one place named after Washington to honor him.
   Write ④ at the beginning of this underlined sentence.

Calculation Boxes

	Reader 1		Reader 2	Reader 3
		Number of Words at Bracket		
		Subtract: Number of Words at Subhead	-130	-220
Number of Words at Bracket		Equals: Number of Words Attempted		
Subtract: Number of Errors	−	Subtract: Number of Errors	−	−
Equals: Words Correct per Minute (WCPM)		Equals: Words Correct per Minute (WCPM)		
Accuracy Percentage	%	Accuracy Percentage	%	%

Mark It!

1. b <u>o l d</u> n e s s
2. r e m i n d e r
3. t h u n d e r b o l t
4. w i l d l i f e
5. b i n d e r
6. s c o l d e d
7. b e h i n d
8. v o l t a g e
9. k i n d n e s s
10. c h i l d p r o o f
11. r e w i n d
12. c o m p o s t

Read It!

1. thunderbolt rewind wildlife
2. behind voltage compost
3. scolded reminder binder
4. childproof boldness kindness
5. compost thunderbolt reminder
6. boldness binder behind
7. kindness childproof voltage
8. wildlife scolded rewind

Each word contains what looks like a Closed Syllable exception with a long vowel, but some of them are actually regular Closed Syllables with short vowels. Write the syllable with the underlined vowel in the correct column. The *schwa* spellings are circled.

CHALLENGING

1. ch<u>i</u>ldhood
2. w<u>i</u>ndow
3. B<u>o</u>st⊙n
4. doorp<u>o</u>st

Long Vowel	Short Vowel
child	

MORE CHALLENGING

5. m<u>i</u>ld⊕st
6. j<u>o</u>lt⊕d
7. ch<u>i</u>ldr⊕n
8. c<u>o</u>stly

Long Vowel	Short Vowel

MOST CHALLENGING

9. c<u>i</u>nderblock
10. mar<u>i</u>g<u>o</u>ld
11. m<u>i</u>ldew
12. gatep<u>o</u>st

Long Vowel	Short Vowel

CHALLENGING

1. boldly asked for a gold ring (6)
2. needs to grind the post down (6)
3. found mold behind the drywall (5)
4. find the mild wind to be peaceful (7)

MORE CHALLENGING

5. ate mild chicken wings while blindfolded (6)
6. soccer ball bounced off of the left goalpost (8)
7. had to childproof most of the kitchen and living room (10)
8. reminded her grandchild how to peel the orange rind (9)

CHALLENGING

1. The small colt felt right at home with the older horses. (11)
2. The wildfire started because of the heat and the dry conditions. (11)
3. My mom planned childish games for my most recent birthday party. (11)
4. If someone is unkind to you, you should forgive them without scolding. (12)

MORE CHALLENGING

5. The gold candleholders are used to hold books in place on the uppermost shelf. (14)
6. How could she possibly hold her grandchild responsible for the broken marigolds? (12)
7. When the binding of my book is falling apart, my teacher finds the clear packing tape to repair it. (19)
8. If you are colorblind, you may not be able to tell the difference between bold colors, such as green and red. (21)

SENTENCES

1. Read each sentence.
2. Underline all of the Closed Syllable exceptions containing the vowel letter **i**.
3. Circle all of the Closed Syllable exceptions containing the vowel letter **o**.
4. Draw a box around all of the words with Closed Syllables that look like exceptions, but have a vowel letter that makes a short vowel sound.

1   Grant had to wear a blindfold when he got dropped off in the easternmost part of the wilderness.

2   The child was asked to wind the window closed because of the wild wind, rain, and bolts of lightning.

3   My oldest sister has been independent since childhood, and she likes to remind me of that.

CHALLENGE YOURSELF

Create sentences using as many words with the given Closed Syllable exceptions as you can.

Example: **ind** - I like to unwind by mindlessly grinding the orange rinds I find on the ground.

1. old - _____

_____

2. ost - _____

_____

Reader 1: _____   Date: _____

Reader 2: _____

Reader 3: _____

Words to Preview	Point & Say
1 **Continental Congress** – a group of delegates from the American colonies who met to discuss how England was unfairly treating them. *The first **Continental Congress** met in 1774 in Philadelphia, Pennsylvania.*	architect
2 **politician** – somebody who is involved in the government or holds a political office. *Jefferson was a successful **politician** who served as governor, vice president, and president.*	declaration
3 **Monticello** – (pronounced mon-ti-chel-o) the home that Thomas Jefferson built. *Many people visit **Monticello** every year to see where Jefferson lived.*	document

Thomas Jefferson

Note: Hyphenated words count as one word.

READER 1

Thomas Jefferson was the third president of the United States. Before	11
that, he was the country's second vice president. Even before that, he	23
played a very important role in American history because he wrote the	35
Declaration of Independence.	38
In 1776, Jefferson was a member of the Continental Congress. He did	50
not like speaking in public and was sometimes called a "silent member"	62
of Congress. But at the age of 33, he was asked to write down why the	78
colonies should break free from Great Britain.	85

READER 2

The document Jefferson wrote stated that America should be independent.	95
That document was called the Declaration of Independence. It was	105
adopted on July 4, 1776. That is why we celebrate the Fourth of July.	119
Today, you can see the document in Washington, DC.	128

Jefferson was much more than just a politician. He was also an architect, 141
a farmer, and an inventor. He drew the plans for his home, a plantation 155
named Monticello, which he built on a mountaintop. There are many 166
items in Monticello that Jefferson invented. 172

READER 3

One thing that Jefferson invented is the Great Clock above the door in 185
the hall of Monticello. This clock does not show time in the same way 199
most clocks do. It uses minute and hour hands to tell time. It also uses 214
cannonballs that hang on both sides of the doorway. They show the day 227
and time by the markings on the wall next to them. 238

One of Jefferson's favorite things to do was farming. His farm had 250
gardens and fruit trees, which provided food for his family. The farm 262
was also a kind of lab to learn about plants. Jefferson rose early every 276
morning to inspect his farm and make notes about his gardens. 287

We know many facts about Thomas Jefferson. Some facts are less 298
well-known than others. For example, many people don't know that 308
he played the violin. He was the first president to have a grandchild 321
born in the White House. He was also governor of Virginia. 332

Jefferson served as president for eight years. He left the White House in 345
1809. The last years of his life were spent at Monticello. In that time, he 360
started the University of Virginia. He died on July 4, 1826. It was the 50th 375
anniversary of the Declaration of Independence. 381

Calculation Boxes

	Reader 1		Reader 2	Reader 3
		Number of Words at Bracket		
		Subtract: Number of Words at Subhead	-85	-172
Number of Words at Bracket		Equals: Number of Words Attempted		
Subtract: Number of Errors	−	Subtract: Number of Errors	−	−
Equals: Words Correct per Minute (WCPM)		Equals: Words Correct per Minute (WCPM)		
Accuracy Percentage	%	Accuracy Percentage	%	%

Reader 1: _____ Date: _____

Reader 2: _____

Reader 3: _____

Thomas Jefferson

Note: Hyphenated words count as one word.

READER 1

Thomas Jefferson was the third president of the United States. Before	11
that, he was the country's second vice president. Even before that, he	23
played a very important role in American history because he wrote the	35
Declaration of Independence.	38
In 1776, Jefferson was a member of the Continental Congress. He did	50
not like speaking in public and was sometimes called a "silent member"	62
of Congress. But at the age of 33, he was asked to write down why the	78
colonies should break free from Great Britain.	85

READER 2

The document Jefferson wrote stated that America should be independent.	95
That document was called the Declaration of Independence. It was	105
adopted on July 4, 1776. That is why we celebrate the Fourth of July.	119
Today, you can see the document in Washington, DC.	128
Jefferson was much more than just a politician. He was also an architect,	141
a farmer, and an inventor. He drew the plans for his home, a plantation	155
named Monticello, which he built on a mountaintop. There are many	166
items in Monticello that Jefferson invented.	172

READER 3

One thing that Jefferson invented is the Great Clock above the door in	185
the hall of Monticello. This clock does not show time in the same way	199
most clocks do. It uses minute and hour hands to tell time. It also uses	214
cannonballs that hang on both sides of the doorway. They show the day	227
and time by the markings on the wall next to them.	238
One of Jefferson's favorite things to do was farming. His farm had	250
gardens and fruit trees, which provided food for his family. The farm	262

was also a kind of lab to learn about plants. Jefferson rose early every	276
morning to inspect his farm and make notes about his gardens.	287

We know many facts about Thomas Jefferson. Some facts are less	298
well-known than others. For example, many people don't know that	308
he played the violin. He was the first president to have a grandchild	321
born in the White House. He was also governor of Virginia.	332

Jefferson served as president for eight years. He left the White House in	345
1809. The last years of his life were spent at Monticello. In that time, he	360
started the University of Virginia. He died on July 4, 1826. It was the 50th	375
anniversary of the Declaration of Independence.	381

Investigate the Text

1 Underline the sentence that tells **how** Jefferson felt about public speaking.
Write ① at the beginning of this underlined sentence.

2 Underline the sentence that tells **where** we can see the Declaration of Independence today.
Write ② at the beginning of this underlined sentence.

3 Underline the sentence that tells **which** instrument Jefferson played.
Write ③ at the beginning of this underlined sentence.

4 Underline the sentence that tells **where** Jefferson lived after he left the White House.
Write ④ at the beginning of this underlined sentence.

Calculation Boxes

	Reader 1		Reader 2	Reader 3
		Number of Words at Bracket		
		Subtract: Number of Words at Subhead	-85	-172
Number of Words at Bracket		Equals: Number of Words Attempted		
Subtract: Number of Errors	–	Subtract: Number of Errors	–	–
Equals: Words Correct per Minute (WCPM)		Equals: Words Correct per Minute (WCPM)		
Accuracy Percentage	%	Accuracy Percentage	%	%

Mark It!

1. val<u>u</u>able
2. area
3. quiet
4. January
5. create
6. triumph
7. medium
8. video
9. poetry
10. triangle
11. obvious
12. idea

Read It!

1. quiet	medium	obvious
2. January	video	poetry
3. triangle	area	create
4. triumph	valuable	idea
5. medium	poetry	triangle
6. valuable	create	quiet
7. obvious	January	area
8. video	idea	triumph

Figure out if the two vowels next to each other are working as a vowel team or if they are split, with each making its own sound. If the vowels are a team, underline them together. If they are split, underline them separately. Place a checkmark in the correct column.

CHALLENGING

1. tri<u>a</u>l
2. trail
3. react
4. deal

Split Vowels	Vowel Team
✓	

MORE CHALLENGING

5. dairy
6. diary
7. creation
8. creature

Split Vowels	Vowel Team

MOST CHALLENGING

9. approach
10. cocoa
11. oasis
12. mosaic

Split Vowels	Vowel Team

CHALLENGING

1. sings a duet and recites a poem (7)

2. picked the bluest peony in the area (7)

3. dial the phone number from your diary (7)

4. heard a baby lion cub meow like a kitten (9)

MORE CHALLENGING

5. did a cameo in the latest pioneer film (8)

6. hilarious reaction to the fake alien video (7)

7. should be a priority for the triangle soloist (8)

8. ate a diet of dandelion greens and ravioli (8)

CHALLENGING

1. One of the benefits of practicing poetry is more fluent reading. (11)

2. The artist created a mosaic of Siamese cats on a large tabletop. (12)

3. I listen to audiobooks when I drive a long distance to my job at the stadium. (16)

4. Arguing and being envious are two things that can make your life less enjoyable. (14)

MORE CHALLENGING

5. Briana earned first place in the geography bee because of her studious habits. (13)

6. Trees are helpful because they absorb carbon dioxide and produce valuable oxygen. (12)

7. The owners reopened the rodeo, but they decided to add Leo, the leotard-wearing lion, to the show. (17)

8. Sophia and Romeo do cardio exercises at their coed gym as a way to get in shape and expend energy. (20)

Create real words using a word part from the first column with a word part from the second column. Write the new word on the line, and then check the box for either Split Vowel or Vowel Team.

Word Parts		New Word	Split Vowel?	Vowel Team?
li	et	_____	☐	☐
		_____	☐	☐
ne	ar	_____	☐	☐
		_____	☐	☐
di	on	_____	☐	☐
		_____	☐	☐
be	al	_____	☐	☐
		_____	☐	☐
re	ad	_____	☐	☐
		_____	☐	☐
		_____	☐	☐
		_____	☐	☐

CHALLENGE YOURSELF

Determine the vowel sound for each vowel in the split vowel. Circle the correct phonemes.

1. **trial**   i = / ī /   or / ē /   a = / ă / or / ə /

2. **duet**   u = / yo͞o / or / o͞o /   e = / ĕ / or / ə /

3. **create** e = / ē /   or / ə /   a = / ā / or / ə /

Reader 1: _____   Date: _____

Reader 2: _____

Reader 3: _____

Words to Preview	Point & Say

1 **Carnival** – a festival held before Lent that is celebrated in many countries.
About two million people celebrate **Carnival** *in Rio de Janeiro every year.*

2 **Holi** – (pronounced the same as holy) an ancient Hindu religious festival.
Holi is also known as the "festival of colors."

3 **La Tomatina** – (pronounced lah toe-muh-tee-nuh) a tomato throwing festival held in Spain.
During **La Tomatina**, *businesses cover their storefronts to make cleanup easier.*

Point & Say

celebrate

celebration

celebrity

Rio De Janeiro

samba (sŏm-buh)

Celebrations

Note: Hyphenated words count as one word.

READER 1

We have something to celebrate this week. We have completed *HD Word!*	12
We have learned so much. These skills will help us for the rest of our lives.	28
Today, you should celebrate your new reading talents.	36
The verb *to celebrate* means to mark a special talent, day, or event.	49
People do this by having celebrations. Celebrations can be parties that	60
mark the joy of finishing a task. They can also mark an important day.	74
These celebrations honor something or someone. The word *celebrity*	83
comes from the verb *to celebrate* as well. *Celebrities* are people who	95
have talents that are *celebrated* by many people. To be *celebrated*	106
means to be admired. Today, you are the *celebrity* who is being	118
celebrated during our reading *celebration*!	123

READER 2

People around the world celebrate in different ways. They celebrate public	134
and religious holidays. They celebrate important events and new talents.	144

Each spring in Brazil, people gather in Rio de Janeiro to celebrate	156
Carnival. The streets are filled with samba music, dancers, costumes,	166
and decorations. The event lasts four days. At the end, there is a parade	190
with many colorful floats. Groups compete to have the best float.	201

Holi celebrates the new spring season and harvest in India. People	212
dress in old clothes. They toss colored powder at each other. Men,	224
women, and children make a colorful mess.	231

READER 3

The Chinese New Year is one of the most important celebrations in	243
China. The people celebrate for 15 days. They wear red clothes. They	255
also set off firecrackers. They gather together for large meals with	266
family. They give children special money for good luck. The event	277
ends with a lantern festival. This includes a dragon dance, costumes,	288
fireworks, and parades.	291

There are many other ways to celebrate throughout the world. In	302
Zambia, the first harvest of the year is remembered with a warrior dance	315
and beef stew. In Turkey, children are celebrated as the future of the	328
nation. Children dress in colorful outfits and perform in plays. In Italy,	340
Carnival is marked with masks and theater. La Tomatina happens in	351
Spain in late August. People throw tomatoes. The city gets covered in	363
tomato paste.	365

Today is a good day to celebrate. It may not be a good idea to throw	381
a tomato in school or toss colored powder at your teacher. However,	393
it is important to mark every victory in your own way, with a little joy	408
and celebration.	410

Calculation Boxes

	Reader 1		Reader 2	Reader 3
		Number of Words at Bracket		
		Subtract: Number of Words at Subhead	-123	-231
Number of Words at Bracket		Equals: Number of Words Attempted		
Subtract: Number of Errors	−	Subtract: Number of Errors	−	−
Equals: Words Correct per Minute (WCPM)		Equals: Words Correct per Minute (WCPM)		
Accuracy Percentage	%	Accuracy Percentage	%	%

Celebrations

Reader 1: _____ Date: _____

Reader 2: _____

Reader 3: _____

Celebrations

Note: Hyphenated words count as one word.

READER 1

We have something to celebrate this week. We have completed *HD Word!*	12
We have learned so much. These skills will help us for the rest of our lives.	28
Today, you should celebrate your new reading talents.	36
The verb *to celebrate* means to mark a special talent, day, or event.	49
People do this by having celebrations. Celebrations can be parties that	60
mark the joy of finishing a task. They can also mark an important day.	74
These celebrations honor something or someone. The word *celebrity*	83
comes from the verb *to celebrate* as well. *Celebrities* are people who	95
have talents that are *celebrated* by many people. To be *celebrated*	106
means to be admired. Today, you are the *celebrity* who is being	118
celebrated during our reading *celebration*!	123

READER 2

People around the world celebrate in different ways. They celebrate public	134
and religious holidays. They celebrate important events and new talents.	144
Each spring in Brazil, people gather in Rio de Janeiro to celebrate	156
Carnival. The streets are filled with samba music, dancers, costumes,	166
and decorations. The event lasts four days. At the end, there is a parade	190
with many colorful floats. Groups compete to have the best float.	201
Holi celebrates the new spring season and harvest in India. People	212
dress in old clothes. They toss colored powder at each other. Men,	224
women, and children make a colorful mess.	231

READER 3

The Chinese New Year is one of the most important celebrations in	243
China. The people celebrate for 15 days. They wear red clothes. They	255
also set off firecrackers. They gather together for large meals with	266
family. They give children special money for good luck. The event	277

ends with a lantern festival. This includes a dragon dance, costumes,	288
fireworks, and parades.	291

There are many other ways to celebrate throughout the world. In	302
Zambia, the first harvest of the year is remembered with a warrior dance	315
and beef stew. In Turkey, children are celebrated as the future of the	328
nation. Children dress in colorful outfits and perform in plays. In Italy,	340
Carnival is marked with masks and theater. La Tomatina happens in	351
Spain in late August. People throw tomatoes. The city gets covered in	363
tomato paste.	365

Today is a good day to celebrate. It may not be a good idea to throw	381
a tomato in school or toss colored powder at your teacher. However,	393
it is important to mark every victory in your own way, with a little joy	408
and celebration.	410

Investigate the Text

1. <u>Underline</u> the sentence that tells **what** the word *celebrated* means.
   Write ① at the beginning of this underlined sentence.

2. <u>Underline</u> the sentence that tells **how long** Carnival is celebrated in Brazil.
   Write ② at the beginning of this underlined sentence.

3. <u>Underline</u> the sentence that tells **what** color is worn during the Chinese New Year.
   Write ③ at the beginning of this underlined sentence.

4. <u>Underline</u> the sentence that tells **what** you should not do in school to celebrate.
   Write ④ at the beginning of this underlined sentence.

Calculation Boxes

	Reader 1		Reader 2	Reader 3
Number of Words at Bracket		Number of Words at Bracket		
		Subtract: Number of Words at Subhead	-123	-231
		Equals: Number of Words Attempted		
Subtract: Number of Errors	−	Subtract: Number of Errors	−	−
Equals: Words Correct per Minute (WCPM)		Equals: Words Correct per Minute (WCPM)		
Accuracy Percentage	%	Accuracy Percentage	%	%

Bingo Card

Clues	Answers
	Write the corresponding card numbers below.
a) Three sounds of *suffix -ed*	
b) Latin chunks	
c) Vowel teams that spell long vowels	
d) Both of the syllables in the word **lakeside**	
e) Open Syllables end with these	
f) Two consonants that make one sound together	
g) Spellings of the first phoneme (sound) in **ouch**	
h) All of the syllables in the word **fantastic**	
i) Vowel team that can spell a long vowel or an "other" vowel phoneme (sound)	
j) Two consonants next to each other that make their own sounds	
k) Closed Syllables end with these	
l) Both of the syllables in the word **floorboard**	
m) The vowels that must follow the letters **c** and **g** to make them spell their soft sounds	
n) Spellings of the first phoneme (sound) in **ooze**	
o) Both of the syllables in the word **trophy**	
p) The vowel phoneme (sound) in the last syllable of the word **vanilla**	
q) Examples of vowel suffixes	
r) Both of the syllables in the word **speedboat**	
s) Examples of consonant suffixes	
t) The last syllables of the words **barnacle**, **rectangle**, and **sample**	

1. Choose one word from each box and create a complete, silly sentence. All three words must be in one sentence, and you will need to add extra words to make your sentence complete. You may also add prefixes and suffixes if you have to.

2. Repeat four more times so you have a total of five complete, silly sentences. Do not use any word more than once.

3. Read your sentences to the class or to a group.

piano	avoid	green
hamburger	smash	cranky
dragon	recycle	oval
homework	celebrate	thankful
igloo	cheer	cloudy
Easter	prevent	jumbo
volcano	ignore	popular
garbage	open	slimy
sunshine	bounce	furry

1. _____

_____

2. _____

_____

3. _____

_____

4. _____

_____

5. _____

_____

Glossary of Terms

Syllable Types

Closed Syllables: syllables with only one vowel, followed by one or more consonants

- **Key info:** The vowel sound in a Closed Syllable is usually short.
- **Examples:**
  - *Single-syllable:*

  - *Multisyllabic:*

Open Syllables: syllables that end with only one vowel letter

- **Key info:** The vowel sound in an Open Syllable is usually long or schwa.
- **Examples:**
  - *Single-syllable:*

  - *Multisyllabic:*

Vowel-Consonant-e Syllables: syllables that end with a vowel letter, a consonant, and a final **e**

- **Key info:**
  - The VCE pattern is one of the most common ways to spell a long vowel sound.
  - VCE Syllables often happen at the end of words.

○ Any vowel letter can be in a VCE Syllable: a_e, e_e, i_e, o_e, u_e, y_e.

- **Examples:**

  ○ *Single-syllable:*

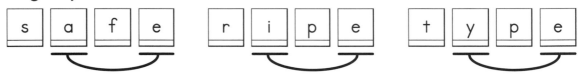

| s | a | f | e | | r | i | p | e | | t | y | p | e |

  ○ *Multisyllabic:*

| cal | cu | late | | com | plete |
| ex | e | cute | | in | spire |

Vowel Team Syllables: syllables with two, three, or four letters that work together to spell one vowel sound

- **Key info:**

  ○ The vowel sound in a Vowel Team Syllable is usually long or other.

  ○ The letters in a vowel team stay together in one syllable.

- **Examples of vowel teams spelling long vowel sounds:**

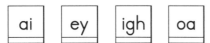

| ai | ey | igh | oa |

- **Examples of vowel teams spelling other vowel sounds:**

| oo | ou | oi | aw |

- **Examples:**

| rea | son | | re | pay | ing | | night | mare |
| with | drew | | en | joy | ment | | ap | plaud |

R-Controlled Syllables: syllables with a vowel letter or vowel team followed by the letter **r**, where the letters combine to spell an r-controlled vowel sound

- **Key info:**
    - R-controlled vowel spellings have two or three letters.
    - /ar/, /or/, and /er/ are r-controlled vowel sounds.
- **Examples of r-controlled vowel spellings:**

ar	or	oor	er	ur	ir

- **Examples:**

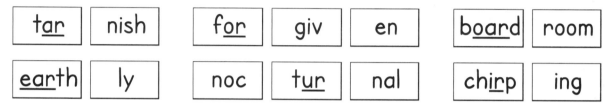

t**ar**	nish		f**or**	giv	en		b**oar**d	room
earth	ly		noc	t**ur**	nal		chi**r**p	ing

Consonant-le Syllables: 3-letter syllables formed by a single consonant letter right before the letters **le**

- **Key info:**
    - Consonant-le Syllables occur only at the end of multisyllabic words.
    - **-le** spells the sounds /uhl/ (schwa plus /l/).
    - **-le** acts like a magnet to pull the consonant before it into the final syllable.
    - Once you decode the Consonant-le Syllable, it is easy to see what type of syllable comes just before it.
- **Examples of consonant-le spellings:** -ble, -cle, -dle, -fle, -gle, -kle, -ple, -tle, -zle
- **Examples:**

puz	**zle**		star	**tle**		cu	bi	**cle**
pud	**dle**		bu	**gle**		re	sem	**ble**

▶ Glossary of Terms

Schwa: /ə/

- is a "lazy" or "reduced" vowel sound because it has less energy than a typical vowel sound;
- is the most common phoneme in English;
- often occurs in multisyllabic words.

- **Key info:**
  - The most common sound for schwa is /uh/, like in **zebra** and **avoid**.
  - The other sound for schwa is /ih/, like in **basket**, **lemon**, and **salad**.
  - Sometimes we need to "flex" a vowel sound to the schwa to pronounce the word correctly.

- **Common schwa spellings:**

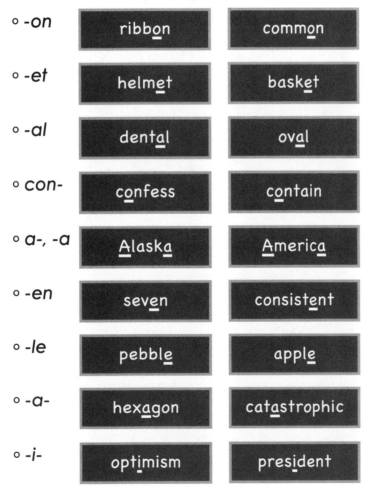

  - *-on*   ribbon   common
  - *-et*   helmet   basket
  - *-al*   dental   oval
  - con-   confess   contain
  - *a-, -a*   Alaska   America
  - *-en*   seven   consistent
  - *-le*   pebble   apple
  - *-a-*   hexagon   catastrophic
  - *-i-*   optimism   president

▶ Glossary of Terms

Reading Multisyllabic Words

➤ When reading longer words:

- Look for the vowel <u>letters</u>.
- Expand your vision to look for the vowel <u>spellings</u>.

➤ First ask yourself:

- How many vowels do I see?
- Are they together or apart?

➤ Then ask:

- Do I see a Latin chunk, prefix, suffix, or any other familiar endings or chunks?
- Do I see a vowel-consonant-e?
- Do I see a vowel team?
- Do I see an r-controlled vowel?
- Do I see a consonant-le?

➤ Finally, ask:

- How many vowel spellings are there?
- How many syllables will there be?

➤ Remember:

- Digraphs always stay together, but blends can be split down the middle. (e<u>s</u>-<u>t</u>a<u>b</u>-<u>lish</u>, qui<u>ck</u>-ly, <u>c</u>om-<u>p</u>lex)
- Doubled consonants are split down the middle. (pu<u>z</u>-<u>z</u>le, a<u>p</u>-<u>p</u>roach)
- When a vowel is by itself, not next to another vowel, it is usually the only vowel in the syllable. (f<u>a</u>n-t<u>a</u>s-t<u>i</u>c, W<u>i</u>s-c<u>o</u>n-s<u>i</u>n, <u>e</u>-l<u>e</u>c-tr<u>i</u>-c<u>a</u>l)
- Vowel teams almost always stay together. (<u>sea</u>-son, m<u>ai</u>n-t<u>ai</u>n, a-st<u>ou</u>nd-ing)
- Vowels followed by an r almost always combine to spell an r-controlled vowel sound. (b<u>ur</u>-den, fl<u>oor</u>-b<u>oar</u>d, f<u>or</u>-bid-den)

- Prefixes and suffixes are often syllables. They stay on one *SyllaBoard*™. The vowel suffixes **-able** and **-ible** each have two vowel spellings and are each split between two *SyllaBoards*™. (<u>dis</u>-a-gree-<u>ment</u>, <u>re</u>-read, <u>un</u>-e-vent-<u>ful</u>, val-u-<u>a-ble</u>, <u>in</u>-flex-<u>i-ble</u>)

- If you see **-le** at the end of a word, it usually grabs the previous consonant and becomes a Consonant-le Syllable. (**jun-<u>gle</u>, pur-<u>ple</u>, fiz-<u>zle</u>**)

- The letters in Latin chunks (**tion, sion, ture**) work together to spell consistent sounds. They stay on one *SyllaBoard*™. (**fic-<u>tion</u>, ad-mis-<u>sion</u>, fix-<u>ture</u>**)

Common Vowel Spellings:

🔊 Long a

Most common: a (Open Syllable), a_e, ay, ai

🔊 Long e

Most common: e (Open Syllable), e_e, ee, ea, y

Less common: ie, ey

🔊 Long i

Most common: i (Open Syllable), i_e, y, igh

Less common: y_e

🔊 Long o

Most common: o (Open Syllable), o_e, oa, ow

🔊 Long u

Most common: u (Open Syllable), u_e

🔊 /or/ as in fork

Most common: or

Less common: our, ore, oor, oar

Glossary of Terms

- **/ar/ as in barn**

  Most common: ar

- **/er/ as in bird**

  Most common: er, ir, ur

  Less common: ear, ar, or

- **/$\overline{oo}$/ as in ooze**

  Most common: oo, u_e, ew, u

- **/ou/ as in ouch**

  Most common: ou, ow

- **/oi/ as in oink**

  Most common: oi, oy

- **/$\breve{oo}$/ as in book**

  Most common: oo

  Less common: u

- **/aw/ as in awesome**

  Most common: au, aw

Common Chunks and Endings

- Identifying prefixes, suffixes, Latin chunks, and other chunks in a word can help you decode the word more quickly.
- When you see one of these groups of letters in a word:
  - Read them as one chunk that almost always spells the same sounds.
  - Keep them together in the same syllable.
  - Once you have decoded the chunk, it is usually easier to figure out the syllable type of the syllable that comes before the chunk.

Glossary of Terms

Common chunks:	all	ing				
Vowel-ng chunks:	ang	ing	ong	ung		
Vowel-nk chunks:	ank	ink	onk	unk		
Latin chunks:	tion	sion	ture			
Consonant Suffixes:	-s	-less	-ness	-ment	-ful	-ly
Vowel Suffixes:	-ed	-es	-ing	-er	-est	-ous
	-y	-able	-ible			
Prefixes:	dis-	con-	un-	im-	in-	re-
	pre-	pro-				

Latin Chunks

- Key info:

  - Latin chunks are groups of letters that work together as whole units, or "chunks," to spell consistent sounds.

  - These chunks only occur in multisyllabic words.

  - When you see a Latin chunk in a word, first separate the chunk from the rest of the word. It is then easier to decode the remaining syllables in the word.

  - Latin chunk **tion** spells /shun/. (**na-tion, va-ca-tion**)

  - Latin chunk **sion** spells /shun/ (**ses-sion, com-pre-hen-sion**) or /zhun/ (**vi-sion, ex-plo-sion**).

  - Latin chunk **ture** spells /cher/. (**na-ture, fea-ture**)

- Examples:

▶ Glossary of Terms

Hard and Soft c and g

- Key info:
  - The letters **c** and **g** can each spell two sounds, a hard sound and a soft sound.
  - *Hard **c*** is /k/ as in **can**, and *soft **c*** is /s/ as in **city**.
  - *Hard **g*** is /g/ as in **gulp**, and *soft **g*** is /j/ as in **gel**.
  - When followed by **e**, **i**, or **y**, **c** and **g** usually spell their soft sounds.
  - When followed by any other vowel letter, **c** and **g** usually spell their hard sounds.
  - When followed by a consonant, **c** and **g** usually spell their hard sounds.
- Examples:
  - *Hard c and g:*

  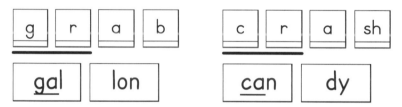

  - *Soft c and g:*

  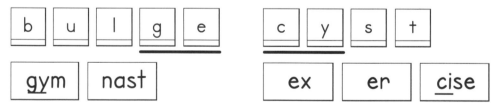

Closed Syllable Exceptions

- Key info:
  - Closed Syllable exceptions look like Closed Syllables, but the vowel letters do not spell the short vowel sounds we expect.

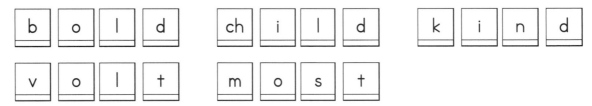

- The vowel sound in a Closed Syllable exception is long.
- The five Closed Syllable exceptions are **old**, **ild**, **ind**, **olt**, and **ost**.

- Examples:

| b | o | l | d |

| ch | i | l | d |

| k | i | n | d |

| v | o | l | t |

| m | o | s | t |

Split Vowels

- Key info:

  - Split vowels are two vowels next to each other that spell two separate vowel sounds.

  - Sometimes split vowels look like a common vowel team (**ai, oa, oi**), and sometimes they do not (**eo, ua, io**).

  - When you see two vowels next to each other in a word, they often work together as a vowel team to spell one vowel phoneme, but sometimes they are split into two different syllables because each one spells its own vowel phoneme.

  - The letter **i** in a split vowel sometimes spells the *long e* sound (**ra-di-o, glor-i-ous**). If it does not work to read the letter **i** as *long i* or *schwa*, try *long e* next.

- Examples:

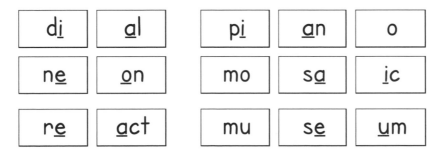

di	al
ne	on
re	act

pi	an	o
mo	sa	ic
mu	se	um

▶ Tracking Chart

Date										
Reader 1										
Reader 2										
Reader 3										
Accuracy % Goal: 98% or better	%	%	%	%	%	%	%	%	%	%
100%										
99%										
98%										
97%										
96%										
95%										
94%										
93%										
92%										
91%										
90% or below										
Words Correct per Minute (WCPM)										
140 or above										
135–139										
130–134										
125–129										
120–124										
115–119										
110–114										
105–109										
100–104										
95–99										
90–94										
85–89										
80–84										
75–79										
70–74										
65–69										
60–64										
55–59										
50–54										
45–49										
below 40										

Tracking Chart

Date									
Reader 1									
Reader 2									
Reader 3									
Accuracy % Goal: 98% or better	%	%	%	%	%	%	%	%	%
100%									
99%									
98%									
97%									
96%									
95%									
94%									
93%									
92%									
91%									
90% or below									
Words Correct per Minute (WCPM)									
140 or above									
135–139									
130–134									
125–129									
120–124									
115–119									
110–114									
105–109									
100–104									
95–99									
90–94									
85–89									
80–84									
75–79									
70–74									
65–69									
60–64									
55–59									
50–54									
45–49									
below 40									

98% WAY TO GO! 98%

▶ Tracking Chart

Date										
Reader 1										
Reader 2										
Reader 3										
Accuracy % Goal: 98% or better	%	%	%	%	%	%	%	%	%	%
100%										
99%										
98%										
97%										
96%										
95%										
94%										
93%										
92%										
91%										
90% or below										
Words Correct per Minute (WCPM)										
140 or above										
135–139										
130–134										
125–129										
120–124										
115–119										
110–114										
105–109										
100–104										
95–99										
90–94										
85–89										
80–84										
75–79										
70–74										
65–69										
60–64										
55–59										
50–54										
45–49										
below 40										

WAY TO GO! 98% or better ACCURACY PERCENTAGE